Stop Trying To Be A Christian:
Learning to Let Jesus Express His Life Through You

Table of Contents

This is dedicated to the wonderful disciples God has given me the privilege to lock arms with and walk together on the journey. Thank you guys for being such an amazing group. I am grateful for friends who have helped along the way. Phil, thanks for helping me edit. Doug, I appreciate your constant encouragement. I am blessed to have a church board that has given their blessing for me to pursue this project. Thank you men and women for being so kind and understanding. I thank the love of my life, Marcia. We have journeyed together now for 36 years. Her love and encouragement gives me strength.

Unless indicated, all Scriptures used in this text are from The New Living Translation. Tyndale. 2004.

1
God is love

For several years I met every week with a young man who was studying for the ministry. I'll call him Steve. I was discipling Steve. We would read assigned passages in the Bible, then discuss them when we met. We prayed together and asked accountability questions. He soaked the information up like a sponge. He was hungry to learn and appeared to be growing steadily in his faith. Until one day when he stopped by the church, threw his office keys on the desk, announced he was done and jumped in his car to leave town. No explanation. No conversation. He just left in an angry huff. We never saw it coming. I wasn't there when it happened, but one of my staff followed him and when he eventually caught up to him, we learned he had been having an affair and was ready to throw everything away. He left the ministry, divorced his wife and turned his back on the church. It was one of the most painful experiences of my life. One of the things that made it so difficult was that I had no idea anything like that was going on in Steve's life. We talked every week. He shared his heart (or so I thought). We prayed together. He had all the "right" answers when we talked Scripture. But there was a serious disconnect deep in his heart. On the outside, everything looked great, but inside he was dying and behind closed doors his marriage was dying.

As a pastor, I have led many discipleship groups, accountability groups and home Bible study groups. At one point, early in my ministry career, I was leading up to eight a week. Crazy! But I was young and didn't know any better. Those groups all focused on studying the Bible, prayer, giving and other spiritual disciplines. And I hope there was some genuine help that came through them. But as a pastor, I have also done a lot of counseling, often with the same people who were in those groups. And what I know is that in spite of all the good Bible knowledge those wonderful people possessed, when looking beyond the "church compartment", their lives were littered with damaged relationships. There has to be a better way.

Some time ago I began looking at discipleship plans in response to a new membership drive for our denomination. Our church has added a new requirement to anyone who wishes to become a member. They must agree to engage in a discipleship process. Each congregation is responsible to develop their own program, believing that a one-size-fits-all approach will not work. Every congregation ministers to different demographics and their needs are unique to that group, so each church is expected to find, or develop their own plan. It's a positive move because it changes the "success" markers. The matrix for success is shifting from attendance and income, to discipleship movements. As I was searching for a program to implement in our local congregation I discovered that virtually everyone I saw on line was performance based. It seemed the tools to measure one's progress all centered around the spiritual disciplines. So just as I had experienced with the disciples I had trained, spiritual maturity was measured by Bible knowledge, prayer, giving, church attendance, servant ministry and personal evangelistic practices.

Because of past experiences, hopefully a little maturity and a closer look at Jesus' methods with His disciples, I have come to believe our discipleship plan must more closely resemble and reflect the priorities of Jesus. And for Jesus, it was not spiritual disciplines, but relationships. On one occasion, Jesus was asked what He considered to be the greatest commandment. His reply was remarkable. "One of them, an expert in religious law, tried to trap him with this question: 'Teacher, which is the most important commandment in the Law of Moses?' Jesus replied, 'You must love the LORD your God with all your heart, all your soul, and all your mind. This is the first and greatest commandment. A second is equally important: 'Love your neighbor as yourself.' The entire law and all the demands of the prophets are based on these two commandments"—(Matthew 22:35-40). Did you get that last line? Everything hinges on those two statements. If we get those right, everything else will fall into place. And the way I read the New Testament, the second command is how we fulfill the first. In other words, the way we love God, is by loving others. The Apostle John tells us that if we do not love others, then it is impossible for us to love God (1 John 4:20).

Therefore, I believe the heart of a discipleship plan should focus around a person's relationships. The health and strength of our relationship with God is most accurately measured by our interpersonal relationships. Granted, we can't get along with everyone. Sometimes the other person makes a healthy relationship impossible, but as the Apostle Paul said, "Do all that you can to live in peace with everyone"—(Romans 12:18). Do we behave in Christlike ways in our relationships, regardless of how others act? Are we fully present to those around us? Are we quick to forgive? Generous? Kind? How we navigate around friends and family is a crucial indicator of our spiritual maturity, and says far more about us than how well we observe our spiritual disciplines. We may, for example, be able to memorize vast amounts of Scripture, but that has little bearing on how we get along with our kids. Our family life is a far more accurate reading of our spiritual temperature than having a bunch of Bible knowledge. It's all about relationships.

God's two big commandments are to love Him with everything we are, and to love others as much as we love ourselves. But here's the problem; on our own, we can't do that. We have no love in and of ourselves to give. All love comes from God, and so before we can even love God or others, we have to first understand how much He loves us (1 John 4:19). That's where we have to start, with God's love for us. The Bible says "God showed ***his great love*** for us by sending Christ to die for us while we were still sinners" (Romans 5:8 emphasis added). "For ***God loved the world*** so much that he gave his one and only Son, so that everyone who believes in him will not perish but have eternal life" (John 3:16 emphasis added). Then The Apostle John simply, but profoundly states, "God is love" (1 John 4:8, 16).

All of these verses speak of the love of God—"His great love", "He loved the world", and "God is love." They reveal the heart of Christianity. To speak of God as being love is not a side issue. It reveals the very DNA of God. God is many things; He is all-powerful, all-knowing, everywhere present. God is holy, just, pure. God is spirit and God is light. Volumes are written on the attributes and qualities of God. But what is God made of? If we cold get to the very center of His nature, what would it be? That is what I am driving at in this chapter.

At His core, God is love. If we can get ahold of that, it will change our lives. There is nothing more important than this truth.

Karl Barth was considered the greatest theologian of the 20th century. He certainly was the most prolific, with his 10,000-page tome, *Church Dogmatics*. Barth, was a Swiss theologian, who during the Second World War, was part of the Confessing Church. This was the group that tried to stop Adolf Hitler. In 1962 Barth was touring the United States, lecturing at universities. During a question and answer session at the University of Chicago, he was asked by a student to summarize his life's work in theology in one sentence. Without hesitation, Barth answered, "Yes, in the words of a song I learned at my mother's knee: 'Jesus loves me, this I know, for the Bible tells me so.'" [1] Though considered a children's hymn, it declares the most important truth in the entire world.

Jesus loves us, because, because… Why does He love us? Is it because we are so great? You know that's not true. If we were so wonderful, we wouldn't have killed His only Son. And don't for a minute think we would have been any different than that rabble that shouted for His death. I know the stuff that goes on inside my brain and if you could take a front row seat to view my thoughts, you wouldn't like me very much. But let me clue you in, if the roles were reversed, I wouldn't like you very much either. What is it about us that makes God love us? Nothing. Absolutely nothing. God loves us because God is love. That's it. There's nothing in us that merits His affection. He initiates the love and it flows toward us because that is who He is. Nothing compelled him to love. It's like the Sun. Nothing compels the Sun to shine. It shines because that's what the Sun does. God loves because that is what He does. He loves us just as we are; sin, wrinkles, flaws and all. He doesn't require we get cleaned up and then He will love us. If that were the case, we would all be in trouble, because none of us could get clean enough. He loves us in our sin, our distorted, blackened heart condition. Understand, He doesn't love the sin. That's a disease He wants to heal in us, but in our fallen, sinful state, He loves us. While we were His enemies, He loved us. Why? Because God is love.

I'm sorry, but I can't get over that statement—God is love. That blows my mind and it touches something deep in my heart that causes my love and adoration for Him to spring up. We could never exhaust those words, for though only three words, they identify the greatest mystery of the universe. I do, however, want to think about the meaning of those words. We won't ever plumb the depths of them, but what little we do see can be enough to change our lives. However, before we dive into it, I need to say something as a safeguard of sorts. We can say, "God is love," but we cannot reverse the sentence and say, "Love is God." Present culture promotes this false idea. Love is celebrated by itself as a power in the universe; that mysterious "thing" that makes the world go round. Huey Lewis expresses the world's sentiments about love in his song, *"It's The Power of Love,"* popularized in the 1985 movie, *"Back To The Future."*

> The power of love is a curious thing
> Make a one man weep, make another man sing
> Change a heart to a little white dove
> More than a feeling, that's the power of love
>
> Tougher than diamonds, whips like cream
> Stronger and harder than a bad girls dream
> Make a bad one good, mmm make a wrong right
> Power of love will keep you home at night
>
> Don't need money, don't take fame
> Don't need no credit card to ride this train
> It's strong and it's sudden and it's cruel sometimes
> But it might just save your life
> That's the power of love
> That's the power of love
>
> First time you feed it might make you sad
> Next time you feed it might make you mad
> But you'll be glad baby when you've found
> That's the power that makes the world go round[2]

It's a popular idea, but presents love as some kind of invisible power that guides and shapes the universe. That sentimental idea may work in a Hallmark movie, but it is dead wrong, because it makes God out to be an impersonal force.

Any love that is experienced in this world comes from God because His transcendent nature touches all of creation. But what we are talking about is not a force. We are talking about a person. God is a person, but if we were to describe this person, His nature, His essence, His Being, we would say, "God is love." I wanted to take a moment and clarify that because as we examine the statement, "God is love," I want to actually look at those words in reverse order—love…is…God. But again, to reverse the words as a sentence is not true. The reason, however, I want to look at the words in reverse order is because I believe it will strengthen the impact.

God Is *Love*

Let's begin with the word love—"God is ***love***." The Greek word John chooses is *agape*. It means kindness and benevolence, but that alone doesn't define God's love. We get a clearer picture of God's love by looking at how the word is used in various contexts. Here are some of the ideas *agape* expresses.

Agape love gives. In the same way we can't play catch without someone to receive the ball; *agape* love requires an object to receive it. There must be one who loves and one who is loved. If love is the DNA of God, and God is eternal, then that means God has always loved. But if love takes two, then whom did God love before He created us? The Apostle John recorded Jesus' prayer on the eve of His arrest. Jesus revealed in His prayer the answer to our question. "Father, I want these whom you have given me to be with me where I am. Then they can see all the glory you gave me because ***you loved me even before the world began***!" (John 17:24 emphasis added). The Father loved Jesus before the world was created. In the beginning, before there was anything, there was God and God is expressed in three Persons; the

Father, the Son and the Holy Spirit. *Agape* love was shared within the Divine Trinity. Richard Rohr calls it, "the divine dance."[3]

God shared His love perfectly within the Triune Godhead. He did not create man or angel because He needed us, nor was He lacking in any way. He enjoyed the fellowship of perfect love between the members of the Godhead. But *Agape* love desires to give. God gave and received love within the members of the Trinity, but the desire of the Triune God was to express His love beyond the bounds of the Trinity. God is also infinite, which means that whatever He is, He is to an unlimited degree. If God is love, and love gives, then God desires to give to an infinite degree. He wanted to share his love with us to the fullest extreme, so beyond the fellowship we would enjoy with God, He determined within His own council to share His love to the point of sacrificing Himself for us (Revelation 13:8).

That tells us another thing about God's love; it is sacrificial. "For God loved the world so much that ***he gave his one and only Son***, so that everyone who believes in him will not perish but have eternal life" (John 3:16 emphasis added). "But God showed his great love for us by sending Christ to die for us while we were still sinners" (Romans 5:8). He expressed love to the ultimate degree by sacrificing Himself for our sake. God could have chosen any number of paths to express His love for us, but He chose the plan that required Him to give to the fullest extent. There is no greater sacrifice than to lay down one's life. That's the path God chose. He took love to the farthest degree possible. If He did not spare His only Son for our sake, then what limit can we place on His love, for nothing is greater than that. In addition to that, we were as unworthy of His love as we could be, which further displays the magnitude of his love, for as Paul wrote, we were His enemies when he died for us. We did nothing to merit His sacrifice.

It is that truth that underscores the reality that God's love is unconditional. "For since our friendship with God was restored by the death of his Son ***while we were still his enemies***, we will certainly be saved through the life of his Son" (Romans 5:10 emphasis added). There is not one good thing in any of us that merits God's love. He does not love us because we are so lovable or because we can somehow make ourselves worthy of His love. We are totally unworthy, yet He lavishes His very best on us.

When Jesus preached the Sermon on the Mount, He said, "You have heard the law that says, 'Love your neighbor' and hate your enemy. But I say, love your enemies! (Matthew 5:43-44a). Jesus is God and He is commanding us to love our enemies. God is not a hypocrite. He would not expect us to do something that He Himself is not willing to do! He wants us to love our enemies, so certainly He will do the same.

In the parable of the prodigal son, we often focus on the younger brother who demanded his inheritance and squandered it on riotous living. Even though he was undeserving, the father received him back into his home. We often hear that parable applied to our lives by saying no matter how far we run away from God, He will receive us back with open arms. That's good news and one of the takeaways from the story, but it is not the main point. Some have suggested the point of the parable is actually the heart condition of the older brother. He was upset that his younger brother received such affection from his father, when his faithful service never got him so much as a steak dinner. He represents the religious person who faithfully jumps through all the right hoops. He is proud of his spiritual superiority, and looks on the world with disdain. Jesus' story was a rebuke to him—perhaps to us. But I think Jesus was getting at something else as well. The real focus was on the father. The younger son demanded his inheritance, which was a backhanded way of saying he wished the father would hurry up and die. Yet when the prodigal returned home, he wasn't able to get two words of his rehearsed apology speech out before the father was hugging and kissing him. In fact, when the father saw him from afar, he hiked up his robes and sprinted toward his son—a very undignified thing to do. But his love for his lost son burst forth with disregard for how he would look to others. Both sons had their issues, but no matter. The father loved them both. That's the point—the father's love. Whether we are the prodigal who runs from God, or the religious hypocrite, God opens His arms wide to us. If He loved us while we were His enemies, then how much more will He love us now that His Son has died for us.

Because God is love and God is eternal, that means His love is eternal. God's love is not turned on and off like a switch. We see love as temporary, as evidenced by the 51% divorce rate. But God's love is not that way—He loved us and called us when we were His enemies. "Many of the people of Israel are now enemies of the Good News, and this benefits you Gentiles. Yet they are still the people he loves because he chose their ancestors Abraham, Isaac, and Jacob. ***For God's gifts and his call can never be withdrawn***" (Romans 11:28-29 emphasis added). Whomever God calls, stays called. He will never revoke His call. That means God will not change His mind about us. We can't make God stop loving us, because His love for us is not based on anything in us. His love for us flows out of His nature, which is Love.

The Apostle Paul understood that, and that's why He made such outlandish statements. "And I am convinced that nothing can ever separate us from God's love. Neither death nor life, neither angels nor demons, neither our fears for today nor our worries about tomorrow—not even the powers of hell can separate us from God's love. No power in the sky above or in the earth below—indeed, nothing in all creation will ever be able to separate us from the love of God that is revealed in Christ Jesus our Lord" (Romans 8:38-39). God is ***LOVE***.

God *Is* Love

Next we need to look at the word "is"—"God ***IS*** love." This does not mean that love is a quality, characteristic or attribute of God. He does not possess love. This is talking about His nature. I can say to you that I have a bottle of water, but it is entirely different than if I say I am a bottle of water. The first statement talks about what I possess. The second statement talks about nature—what I am. When John wrote God is love, he did not mean that God possessed love, like it was one of His qualities or attributes. God doesn't possess love. God is love. This is speaking of His essence, His very being.

"Is" is a present tense word, which means God's love is always now. When Moses asked God His name, He replied, "I AM WHO I AM" (Exodus 3:14). That word means God is the one who was, the one who is and the one who always shall be. It's past, present and future all wrapped up in one—representing Him who is beyond time and lives in the ever present now. That idea is reflected and celebrated around the throne of God as the angelic creatures proclaim, "Holy, holy, holy is the Lord God, the Almighty—the one who always was, who is, and who is still to come" (Revelation 4:8). God is always in the present now. Because God is love, His love is always present. He has always loved us, He does love us and He always will love us.

"Is" tells us that all God's attributes must be understood in light of His love. Because God doesn't just possess love, but is love, then any quality He expresses must flow through His nature. For example, one of God's attributes is omnipotence. That means God is all-powerful and can do whatever He chooses. That attribute, however, is always expressed through His nature, which is love. If God were not love, but was swayed by lustful passions, like the pagan gods, then His omnipotence would be a frightening thing. We can trust Him, however, because even though He possesses all power and could literally squash the universe in His hands, we know He will always act in accordance with His nature, which is love.

Let's think about an attribute that appears most unlike love—wrath. At times God expresses wrath. That seems very unloving, and even hateful. But because God is love, and doesn't just simply possess love, then even wrath must be understood as coming through His loving nature.

In his book, *Saints in the Arms of a Happy God*, Jeff Turner tells a story about when he was a boy. He and his buddies enjoyed knocking over dead trees in the woods near his home. One day they saw a giant tree that was clearly dead and ready to topple over. It was the perfect invitation to land a flying drop kick. One of his friends hit the tree square and knocked it over. But when he did, swarming hornets attacked him. They raced back home to escape the attack. His friend, Trevor, who got the worst of it, ran into his house screaming for his dad. Jeff and his other friend stayed outside. They heard the father yelling and soon slapping their friend. They cringed, thinking he was beating his son for doing such a stupid thing. But as they listened further, they realized the slaps were not punishment, but rather the dad was trying to kill the hornets that were still attacking his son. What sounded at first like an act of punishment was really an act of love.[4]

What looks like wrath is actually love. When the bloodthirsty mob was gathered around the cross, they hurled insults that cut deeply into Jesus' heart. They believed God was punishing Him. They reasoned only someone deserving God's judgment would hang on a Roman cross. Isaiah peered down through the ages and with prophetic voice predicted, "we considered him punished by God, stricken by him, and afflicted" (Isaiah 53:4c NIV). The people thought God was punishing Jesus for His sins. We don't believe that. We know He was innocent of all sin.

Instead, we have believed that God was punishing Him for our sins. But when we look more closely, we see the love of the Father working with the Son and the Holy Spirit to rescue man from sin, death and Satan. God's wrath was not against the Son, but the wrath of the Father, the Son and the Spirit were all together against sin. Jesus was not being punished on the cross. The triune God was working out His plan to destroy sin. Jesus took the sin of the world into Himself to end its reign over humanity. What looks like wrath is actually love. In love, the Godhead is destroying sin. We will look at this in greater depth in another chapter.

"Is" tells us that all God's activities are centered around His nature, which is love. Not only are God's attributes characterized by God's love, but every action He takes flows through that filter. When God disciplines us, He does it because of love (Hebrews 12:5-9). Jesus confronted Peter after His resurrection. On the night of His trial, Peter had denied three times that he knew the Lord. He had boasted he would die for the Lord, but at the crucial moment, Peter betrayed his best friend. In their first face to face meeting after Jesus' resurrection, Jesus asked Peter three times if Peter loved Him. It's hard to miss the connection to Peter's three denials.

The first time Jesus asked Peter if he loved him, He used the word *agape*. Before Jesus' arrest, Peter had said he would die for the Lord; that he would selflessly give himself up. That's *agape* love. Peter was wrong and Jesus' question forced him to face it. The second time, Jesus said the same thing. The third time, however, Jesus used a different word. He used the word *Phileo*. That's the Greek word that means brotherly love. It's as if Jesus was saying, "Peter, we've established you do not *agape* me. But Peter, do you even *Phileo* me? Do you even love me as a friend?" Peter was grieved when Jesus asked him the third time.

Blow after blow, Jesus was confronting Peter's sin. That looks like stern judgment and discipline. In fact, to add salt to the wound, Jesus built a charcoal fire on the beach where they met. The only other place where we see a charcoal fire mentioned is in the courtyard of the High Priest at the very place, and on the very night Peter denied the Lord. It's like Jesus was recreating the scene in order to confront His betrayal. It doesn't look very loving. But if we examine the story closely, we will notice that each time Jesus asked Peter if he loved him and Peter tried to give a satisfactory answer, Jesus commissioned Peter to "Feed my sheep" (John 21:15-19).

At the very moment Jesus was exposing Peter's sin, He was reinforcing his call. He was asking Peter to continue in his mission. In fact, the story began by the disciples catching such a huge cache of fish their nets couldn't hold them. That same miracle happened at the beginning of Jesus' ministry when he called His disciples to follow Him. He had said to Peter, "follow me and I will make you fishers of men" (Mark 1:17). The two miracles formed bookends to Jesus' ministry. It's as if He was saying, "Yes you blew it. Let's admit that. But I called you at the beginning of my ministry and my heart has not changed. You're the one I want—sins and all." Even when God disciplines us, He does so in love. God's love for us and His calling of us is without repentance or regret.

God Is Love

Finally, let's examine the word, God—"***GOD*** is love." When we think of God, we need to think of Jesus. Sometimes we see God as the "good cop, bad cop," with the Old Testament God being the bad cop and the New Testament God being the good cop. The truth is, Jesus is the perfect representation of the Father. The Biblical record states it clearly, "The Son radiates God's own glory and expresses the very character of God" (Hebrews 1:3).

In the upper room, Jesus asked, " 'Have I been with you all this time, Philip, and yet you still don't know who I am? Anyone who has seen me has seen the Father! So why are you asking me to show him to you? Don't you believe that I am in the Father and the Father is in me? The words I speak are not my own, but my Father who lives in me does his work through me. Just believe that I am in the Father and the Father is in me. Or at least believe because of the work you have seen me do' " (John 14:9-11). The Apostle Paul wrote, "Christ is the visible image of the invisible God. He existed before anything was created and is supreme over all creation" (Colossians 1:15). We cannot draw distinctions between Jesus and the Father. Everything Jesus did and said was a manifestation of His Father's will (John 5:19; 12:49).

When the Roman soldiers were driving the spikes through His wrists, Jesus prayed, "Father forgive them" (Luke 23:34). His prayer was not an attempt to convince a reluctant God who was standing on the edge of heaven about to unleash His furry on the Romans to stand down. No, the Father wanted the Son to pray those words. When Jesus prayed them, the soldiers did not repent. They had no thoughts of Jesus, other than He was a criminal deserving death. They drove that hammer with the same force as they did with any other piece of filth that was being crucified that day. They weren't seeking forgiveness, nor would they have cared one bit whether or not Jesus forgave them. They didn't ask for forgiveness. They didn't seek it, but Jesus offered it. And because Jesus and the Father are one, the Father offered it as well. Jesus forgave them without being asked, which means the Father forgave them without being asked. We can say that with confidence, because the Father is exactly like Jesus.

Exhausted from tending to the needs of the masses, Jesus slipped away for a time of rest. But the people tracked Him down, not caring about His well-being. All they cared about was their personal pain and the hope that Jesus cold relieve it. They used Him. Even so, when Jesus saw their desperation, He felt compassion for them. His heart was touched by the poverty, sickness and broken lives He saw

(Mark 6:34; Matthew 9:36; 15:32). That means the Father felt the exact same way.

Jesus allowed a prostitute to wash His feet with her hair. He spent time with drunks. He touched lepers when He healed them. He called children to sit on His lap. He went out of his way to dine with tax collectors—some of the most despised people in that society. Jesus loved people that most would want to avoid; the people on the margins. But if He loved them, then it means the Father loved them too.

On another occasion, Jesus deliberately defied the authorities and broke the Sabbath law. "And it came about on another Sabbath, that He entered the synagogue and was teaching; and there was a man there whose right hand was withered" (Luke 6:6). This was on the heels of a confrontation Jesus had with the religious rulers, only a few days earlier. His disciples had been eating grain while walking through a field on the Sabbath. The authorities realized He was loose with the rules, so were watching Him to catch Him in a crime serious enough that they could arrest Him. Jesus knew what they were doing, and He realized they were placing the regulations of the law above the needs of the people. His mission was to heal the hurting, but from this incident it is clear He also wanted to shatter the religious leader's legalistic stranglehold on the people. To that end, Jesus intentionally chose Sabbaths to do His work. He wanted to challenge their ridiculous rules.

The story says, "There was a man there whose right hand was withered" (Luke 6:6). The word withered literally means all dried up. The tense of the Greek word indicates this happened to the man some time ago. Most likely it was the result of an accident, injury or disease. Jesus saw this man and was moved with compassion—not only because his hand was deformed, but because in that culture, the man couldn't work, couldn't provide for his family, and there was nothing like insurance or medical help in that day. Jesus hurt for the man. Notice, however, how the Pharisees responded to this man's presence. "And the scribes and the Pharisees were watching Him closely, to see if He healed on the Sabbath, in order that they might find reason to accuse Him" (Luke 6:7). They were lurking with sinister intent. They didn't care a bit about the crippled man. They were just waiting to pounce on Jesus if He broke the rules.

The gospel says, "they questioned Him, saying, 'Is it lawful to heal on the Sabbath?' " (Matthew 12:10b). Luke tells us that Jesus knew exactly what they were thinking (Luke 6:8). In defiance of the Pharisees, Jesus had the man step to the front of the synagogue, so everyone could see him. He could have avoided all this by healing the man the next day, or healing him privately, but He deliberately chose to deal with this in public on the Sabbath. He didn't do it to be rebellious. He did it because Jesus always put people first. Legalists don't do that. They put rules first. Jesus prefaced the miracle by putting the Pharisees' cold hearts on display. "And He said to them, 'What man shall there be among you, who shall have one sheep, and if it falls into a pit on the Sabbath, will he not take hold of it, and lift it out? Of how much more value then is a man than a sheep!' " (Matthew 12:11-12a).

He knew what they were thinking, so He questioned them accordingly. He asked them in the presence of everyone if it was lawful to do good on the Sabbath (like He was intending to do), or to do harm on the Sabbath (like they wanted to do). He asked if it was good to save a life (like He was going to do), or to kill (like they wanted to do to Him). (Mark 3:4). But they kept silent. They knew they were on the spot. I think Jesus glared at them because He wanted the tension to mount. It was an awkward, painful silence. After looking around at them, He asked the man to stretch out his hand in front of everyone, and then He healed him (Mark 3:5a; Matthews 12:13b).

Do you know what makes Jesus angry? It's not people who break a few rules. It's legalists who don't care about people. Instead of rejoicing that the man's hand was healed and that he could now provide for his family, they were filled with rage (Luke 6:11a). In fact, Mark's gospel tells us, "the Pharisees went out and immediately began taking counsel with the Herodians against Him, as to how they might destroy Him" (Mark 3:6).

Jesus put people first, even if it meant breaking the rules. He was interested in meeting people's needs. If God is exactly like Jesus, then that means the Father responds to us in the same exact way. Have we failed God? So did Peter, and Jesus sought him out to restore him. The Father, through the Spirit seeks us out to restore what is hurting in our souls as well. Do we have doubts? So did the man with the demonized son. When Jesus asked the father if he believed, the father responded, "I do believe, but help my unbelief." That guy had faith and doubt all mixed up in his heart at the same time. But do you know what Jesus did? He took compassion on him and healed the boy, in spite of the father's doubts. If Jesus did that for him, He will do it for us. And if Jesus is that way towards us, then so is the Father.

Do we repeat the same sins over and over? So did the disciples. They constantly were arguing over who was the greatest. They repeatedly stumbled in their faith. They abandoned the Lord in His time of need. They messed up over and over, but Jesus loved them in spite of their repeated failures and used them to build His church. Jesus feels that way about us, as well, and if Jesus feels about us, then so does the Father, because the Father is exactly like Jesus.

Life Changing Implications

God is love! That truth can change us. That reality has incredible implications for our lives. When we understand that God is love, it motivates us to love. Jesus wanted His disciples to get that. He prayed that they would understand who the Father really is, because He knew that knowledge would open their hearts to receive the Father's love. "O righteous Father, the world doesn't know you, but I do; and these disciples know you sent me. *I have revealed you to them, and I will continue to do so. Then your love for me will be in them*, and I will be in them" (John 17:25-26 emphasis added). Once we understand His love for us, that love flows out through us toward others. "We love each other because he loved us first" (1 John 4:19).

When we understand that God is love, it motivates us to live holy lives. When some people hear that God's love is selfless, sacrificial, unconditional and eternal, they get nervous that people will run toward sin and throw away all moral restraint. Nothing could be further from the truth. God's love comes to us as grace and mercy. Grace is the positive side where God gives us what we don't deserve. Mercy is the negative side where God withholds what we do deserve. The Bible is clear that grace motivates and empowers us to live godly lives. "For the grace of God has appeared, bringing salvation to all men, ***instructing us*** to deny ungodliness and worldly desires and to live sensibly, righteously and godly in the present age" (Titus 2:11-12 NASB emphasis added). According to that verse, God's grace instructs us, it teaches us, it compels us to live godly lives.

His mercy does the same thing. "Don't you see how wonderfully kind, tolerant, and patient God is with you? Does this mean nothing to you? Can't you see that his kindness is intended to turn you from your sin?" (Romans 2:4). God's tolerance and patience is the expression of mercy. That kindness, rather than igniting our lustful passions because we have permission to sin with freedom, actually motivates us to do just the opposite. In fact, anyone who uses the freedom they have in Christ to excuse sinful living has not actually understood the true nature of God's love.

If this teaching on grace causes people to be concerned that I am overstating the case to the point that people may think they can live anyway they want to, then I say I am just arriving at where I should be. I am walking in the footsteps of the Apostle Paul, whose grace teachings elicited a similar complaint. Here is how he responded to such charges. "God's law was given so that all people could see how sinful they were. But as people sinned more and more, God's wonderful grace became more abundant. So just as sin ruled over all people and brought them to death, now God's wonderful grace rules instead, giving us right standing with God and resulting in eternal life through Jesus Christ our Lord. Well then, should we keep on sinning so that God can show us more and more of his wonderful grace? Of course not! Since we have died to sin, how can we continue to live in it?" (Romans 5:20-6:2). When truly understood God's love is not seen as a license to sin. Just the opposite—it compels us to live for Him.

As I said at the beginning of this chapter, when we understand that God is love, it provides a different way to measure our own spiritual growth. Too often the church measures spiritual maturity by disciplines and rules; prayer, church attendance, Bible reading, refraining from certain sins, like drinking, smoking and cussing. (We conveniently leave out things like gossip and backbiting). But all of these things are performance based. It's all about what we do. But if God is love, then God is about relationships. The measure of our spiritual maturity should be love. In other words, how are our relationships? How is our relationship with our spouse, children, parents, friends, neighbors, co-workers? And how do we measure those?

Is there anything from God's Word that would give us a guide to maturing in our relationships? There is. It's the fruit of the Spirit. The Apostle Paul lists them as the expression of God's nature living through us. There are nine fruit listed, but they are a representation of the multifaceted character of God. One of the key things about the fruit, is that every one has to do with relationships. Each quality is a description of how God wants to express His love through us into our relationships; love, joy, peace, patience, kindness, goodness, gentleness, faithfulness, self-control (Galatians 5:22-23). The fruit then becomes the matrix through which we measure our spiritual growth.

For example, do we see kindness expressed in our marriage, or friendships, etc.? What are the hurdles that may keep kindness from flowing freely through our lives? How can we address those hurdles and by the power of God's Spirit, see them removed from our lives so that His kindness can flow freely through us? Such questions will enable us to map out a discipleship plan that will help us grow into Christlike followers of God. Part of the journey we will go through in this manual will be to explore those areas of our lives with regards to the fruit of the Spirit, identify the barriers that hinder the Spirit from manifesting His life through us, and seek to allow God to more freely express His love in our relationships.

On one occasion, Paul was writing the church to describe what love looked like. His description is in 1 Corinthians. We could easily say this is what God looks like, for God is love. But have you ever read 1 Corinthians 13 and thought of it—not as a prescription for how we should live (though it is that)—but rather as a description of how God relates to us? Let me share a portion of that chapter, inserting the word God every place the word love appears. It may change your perception of how God relates to you. "GOD is patient and kind. GOD is not jealous or boastful or proud or rude. GOD does not demand HIS own way. GOD is not irritable, and GOD keeps no record of being wronged. GOD does not rejoice about injustice but rejoices whenever the truth wins out. GOD never gives up, GOD never loses faith, GOD is always hopeful, and GOD endures through every circumstance" (1 Corinthians 13:4-7).

2
God Is Exactly Like Jesus

God is like Jesus. God has always been like Jesus. There has never been a time when God was not like Jesus—Brian Zahnd[5]

"Long ago you laid the foundation of the earth and made the heavens with your hands. They will perish, but you remain forever; they will wear out like old clothing. You will change them like a garment and discard them. But **you are always the same**; you will live forever" (Psalm 102:25-27 emphasis added). "I am the Lord, and I do not change" (Malachi 3:6). "Whatever is good and perfect comes down to us from God our Father, who created all the lights in the heavens. **He never changes** or casts a shifting shadow" (James 1:17 emphasis added).

God and Jesus Are the Same

God never changes, but if that's true, how can Jesus and the Father be the same? Jesus is loving, kind and compassionate, while the God portrayed in the Old Testament appears to be stern, violent and condemning. God is perfectly revealed in Jesus, but is Jesus perfectly revealed in the Old Testament? Jesus does not alter God, or modify Him in any way. He manifests God. If that were not true, then He could not claim to be one with the Father (John 10:30). If they were not exactly alike, then Jesus could not have told Philip that to see Him is to see the Father. Jesus shows us what God is like, and though what He reveals may seem like a different God than seen in the Old Testament, it is the same God. Jesus does not present a new God to us, but gives us a clearer vision of how God has been all along. The problem has not been with the Father or the Son, but with our understanding of Him.

"In the beginning the Word already existed. The Word was with God, and the Word was God…So the Word became human and made his home among us. He was full of unfailing love and faithfulness. And we have seen his glory, the glory of the Father's one and only Son…No one has ever seen God. But the unique One, who is himself God, is near to the Father's heart. He has revealed God to us" (John 1:1, 14, 18).

"Jesus shouted to the crowds, 'If you trust me, you are trusting not only me, but also God who sent me. For when you see me, you are seeing the one who sent me.'" (John 12:44-45).

"Philip said, 'Lord, show us the Father, and we will be satisfied.' Jesus replied, 'Have I been with you all this time, Philip, and yet you still don't know who I am? Anyone who has seen me has seen the Father! So why are you asking me to show him to you?'" (John 14:8-9).

"So the Jewish leaders tried all the harder to find a way to kill him. For he not only broke the Sabbath, he called God his Father, thereby making himself equal with God. So Jesus explained, 'I tell you the truth, the Son can do nothing by himself. He does only what he sees the Father doing. Whatever the Father does, the Son also does'" (John 5:18-19).

"Christ is the visible image of the invisible God" (Colossians 1:15).

"For in Christ lives all the fullness of God in a human body" (Colossians 2:9).

"The Son radiates God's own glory and expresses the very character of God" (Hebrews 1:3).

Jesus Doesn't Look Like the God of the Old Testament

Scripture is clear that Jesus is exactly like God, but that also means God is exactly like Jesus. Michael Ramsey, Archbishop of Canterbury, said "God is entirely Christlike, and in Him there is no unChristlikeness at all."[6] That immediately creates a problem in our minds, because we look at what Jesus is like, and then we think of what God looks like in the Old Testament, and they don't look like the same person.

God commands violence, vengeance and genocide in the Old Testament, but Jesus rejects violence and teaches mercy and forgiveness toward others, even our enemies. How can Jesus be exactly like God and God be exactly like Jesus if they seem so different? This is not a small issue. The apparent contradiction has been a pebble in the shoe of many Christians. Some have even rejected Christianity because the God presented in the Old Testament is incompatible with Jesus. There are probably many who simply tuck this issue away in some back closet of their conscious mind. But this contradiction can't be so easily dismissed.

We can try to solve this issue by saying Jesus and the Father are not exactly alike. The result, however, is that we end up pitting one against the other, with the Father being the villain and the Son being the hero. The stereotype portrays the Father bent on condemning us all to hell, while the Son steps in to rescue us from the His wrath. That kind of thinking makes the Father someone to fear and avoid. Suddenly we have a schizophrenic God rescuing us from Himself. No, Jesus and the Father are one. They are working for the same thing. Jesus didn't come to save us from the wrath of the Father. Jesus and the Father were united in saving us from sin and death. The Father, the Son and the Holy Spirit worked together in unity, and the Son's death was not because God was punishing Him.

The people around the foot of the cross thought God was punishing Jesus for His sins. Isaiah predicted they would do that. "He was despised and rejected—a man of sorrows, acquainted with deepest grief. We turned our backs on him and looked the other way. He was despised, and we did not care. Yet it was our weaknesses he carried; it was our sorrows that weighed him down. And we thought his troubles were a punishment from God, a punishment for his own sins!"—(Isaiah 53:3-4). We realize that's not what was happening, but we have said something similar—that the Father was punishing Jesus for our sins. It's true, Jesus died for our sins, but the Father was not punishing Him. On the contrary, the Father was cooperating with the Son to destroy our sin. Verse 5 underscores that reality; "But he was pierced for our rebellion, crushed for our sins"—(Isaiah 53:5).

It was all about destroying the power of sin. Here's how the New Testament describes it; "He made Him who knew no sin to be sin on our behalf, so that we might become the righteousness of God in Him"—(2 Corinthians 5:21). "For what the law was powerless to do because it was weakened by the flesh, God did by sending his own Son in the likeness of sinful flesh to be a sin offering. And so he condemned sin in the flesh"—(Romans 8:3). The Father was right there with the Son working for our redemption. "God was reconciling the world to himself in Christ"—(2 Corinthians 5:19).

Even when Jesus cried "My God My God, why have you forsaken me" (Psalm 22:1), it looked like abandonment from the Father, but it was not. Those who heard His words would have known Jesus was quoting the Psalms. It would be similar to me asking you to finish this sentence: "Four score and seven…" We are so familiar with the Gettysburg address that we can finish the first line, if not more. The people of that day could quote the rest of the Psalm. And that was the point. By quoting the first line, "My God, my God, why have you forsaken me?" the people would fill in the rest. The first line goes on to ask, "Why are you so far from saving me?" The writer feels abandoned, but the tension is resolved in verse 24. "For he has not despised or scorned the suffering of the afflicted one; he has not hidden his face from him but has listened to his cry for help"—(Psalm 22:24). Jesus intended them to fill in the blanks. God did not abandon Jesus, though at first glance it may have looked that way.

We Have to Account for Progressive Revelation

The reason for the confusion between the God of the Old Testament and the God of the New Testament, is because of something called progressive revelation. The revealing of God's redemptive plan became clearer as time progressed. In the beginning God shared the redeemer would come through the human race (Genesis 3:15). Once Abraham came on the scene, God narrowed the focus of His redemptive promise to a specific family (Genesis 12:3; 22:18). Later, it was revealed the promised One would come through a specific tribe of Abraham's family (Genesis 49:8-12). Eventually, it was learned the Messiah would be born in Bethlehem (Micah 5:2).

The identity of the Messiah was only one aspect of progressive revelation. The understanding of what God is like was also progressive in nature. Notice, for example, what the Apostle John says about God. "No one has ever seen God. But the unique One, who is himself God, is near to the Father's heart. He has revealed God to us"—(John 1:18). That clearly says that no one has ever seen God. But wait a minute. What about Adam? The Bible clearly states that God talked with Adam in the Garden of Eden after Adam and Eve had eaten from the forbidden tree (Genesis 3:8-9). Moses actually spoke with God face to face (Exodus 33:11). Abraham sat down to dinner with the Lord (Genesis 18:1-8). Jacob wrestled in hand-to-hand combat with God (Genesis 32:22-32). Ezekiel saw the Son of God sitting on His throne (Ezekiel 1:26). We could also speak of Enoch, Elijah, Isaiah and others. How can John say no one has seen God?

It is true those Old Testament forefathers saw God, but they only saw glimpses of Him. They didn't see Him in his fullness; something was always veiled. Moses wanted to see a complete revelation of God and was told he couldn't. "Moses responded, 'Then show me your glorious presence.' The Lord replied, 'I will make all my goodness pass before you, and I will call out my name, Yahweh, before you. For I will show mercy to anyone I choose, and I will show compassion to anyone I choose. But you may not look directly at my face, for no one may see me and live.' The Lord continued, 'Look, stand near me on this rock. As my glorious presence passes by, I will hide you in the crevice of the rock and cover you with my hand until I have passed by. Then I will remove my hand and let you see me from behind. But my face will not be seen" (Exodus 33:18-23).

No on ever saw God in His fullness. That only happened when Jesus came. "Long ago God spoke many times and in many ways to our ancestors through the prophets. And now in these final days, he has spoken to us through his Son" (Hebrews 1:1-2). The people of the Old Testament couldn't fully understand God until Jesus revealed Him.

The Word of God Is More than Ink, It Is a Living Person

The Bible speaks of Jesus as being the Word of God. "In the beginning the Word already existed. The Word was with God, and the Word was God"—(John 1:1). When we speak of the Word of God, do we mean Jesus or the Bible? I suppose we can mean both, but does one supersede the other? Which is greater, the written Word, or the Living Word? Obviously, the Living Word is superior, for the Living Word is Jesus. In fact, the written Word (what we call Scripture) points to the Living Word. Therefore, the lens through which we must interpret the Bible is the Living Word. Jesus made it clear the Scripture is to be interpreted through Him.

On one occasion Jesus confronted the Pharisees about their knowledge of the Scriptures. He said, "You search the Scriptures because you think they give you eternal life. But the Scriptures point to me"—(John 5:39). The Scriptures talk about eternal life, but Jesus is eternal life.

Now, let's go back to the idea that there is a contradiction between the Old Testament God and the New Testament God. We see a loving and kind God in the New Testament, but a God who seems angry and violent in the Old Testament. But if God is exactly like Jesus and Jesus is exactly like God, then there is obviously some kind of a problem. But the problem goes away if we recognize the revelation of God is progressive.

Let's take for example, a "problem passage" in 1st Samuel. "Now the Spirit of the Lord had left Saul, and the Lord sent a tormenting spirit that filled him with depression and fear"—(1 Samuel 16:14). This verse says the Lord sent an evil spirit to tempt Saul. But in the New Testament book of James we read, "And remember, when you are being tempted, do not say, 'God is tempting me.' God is never tempted to do wrong, and he never tempts anyone else"—(James 1:13). Scholars agree that when the evil spirit went to torment Saul, God did not send it or cause it, but He did allow it. At the very least, He did not stop it from happening, because He allows freedom in the world He has created. In fact, the passage in Samuel says the Spirit of the Lord had left Saul. God was removing His protective hand and allowing Saul to reap what he had sown, but the Biblical writer recorded it as if God did it directly. From his perspective, God intentionally sent that evil spirit. But James says that God doesn't do that. That's because James now has a better revelation of the nature of God.

God was progressively revealed more and more until the fullness of time when God was fully revealed in Jesus. That can apply to passages of wrath and judgment as well. For example, the prophets Jeremiah and Isaiah wrote that God sent judgment on Israel by the Babylonians. We know as a matter of history that the Babylonians did conquer and deport Israel. God was aware that it was going to happen and moved His prophets to predict it as a warning. But when the Babylonians attacked Israel they committed horrible atrocities. Was that God's will, or was something else happening?

We get a clearer understanding of how God judges people in the New Testament. The Apostle Paul shows that when God judges a people, He does so by leaving them to reap the natural result of their sins. This lengthy passage in Romans 1 describes the process of God removing His hand of restraint and allowing the downward spiral of sin to destroy a society. Notice the three times it says that God turned the people over to themselves.

"But God shows his anger from heaven against all sinful, wicked people who suppress the truth by their wickedness. They know the truth about God because he has made it obvious to them. For ever since the world was created, people have seen the earth and sky. Through everything God made, they can clearly see his invisible qualities—his eternal power and divine nature. So they have no excuse for not knowing God. Yes, they knew God, but they wouldn't worship him as God or even give him thanks. And they began to think up foolish ideas of what God was like. As a result, their minds became dark and confused. Claiming to be wise, they instead became utter fools. And instead of worshiping the glorious, ever-living God, they worshiped idols made to look like mere people and birds and animals and reptiles. **So God abandoned them to do whatever shameful things their hearts desired**. As a result, they did vile and degrading things with each other's bodies. They traded the truth about God for a lie. So they worshiped and served the things God created instead of the Creator himself, who is worthy of eternal praise! Amen. **That is why God abandoned them to their shameful desires.** Even the women turned against the natural way to have sex and instead indulged in sex with each other. And the men, instead of having normal sexual relations with women, burned with lust for each other. Men did shameful things with other men, and as a result of this sin, they suffered within themselves the penalty they deserved. Since they thought it foolish to acknowledge God, **he abandoned them to their foolish thinking and let them do things that should never be done**. Their lives became full of every kind of wickedness, sin, greed, hate, envy, murder, quarreling, deception, malicious behavior, and gossip. They are backstabbers, haters of God, insolent, proud, and boastful. They invent new ways of sinning, and they disobey their parents. They refuse to understand, break their promises, are heartless, and have no mercy. They know God's justice requires that those who do these things deserve to die, yet they do them anyway. Worse yet, they encourage others to do them, too"—(Romans 1:18-32 emphasis added).

The judgment was that sin was allowed to do what sin does— it destroys. God took His hand of restraint off, and sin did its own destructive work. God didn't judge them directly, but He removed His protective hand and their own sin judged them. Paul stated the principle in his letter to the Galatians. "Those who live only to satisfy their own sinful nature **will harvest decay and death from that sinful nature.** But those who live to please the Spirit will harvest everlasting life from the Spirit"—(Galatians 6:8 emphasis added).

Back to the Babylonians—God didn't directly destroy Israel via the Babylonians, but allowed them to reap what they had sown. Through their sinful choices they rejected God and turned to political allies hoping to fortify themselves against a Babylonian threat. That incited the Babylonians to attack, and Israel reaped what they had sown. But the Bible records it as if God directed and caused it. That's the nature of progressive revelation.

Jesus totally understood this and was careful when quoting Old Testament passages to reflect His nature. For example, when visiting His home synagogue, Jesus was given the opportunity to read the Scriptures and comment on them. He read a portion of Isaiah, but mysteriously stopped reading in the middle of a sentence. He left off at a comma and intentionally stopped reading. "The scroll of Isaiah the prophet was handed to him. He unrolled the scroll and found the place where this was written: 'The Spirit of the Lord is upon me, for he has anointed me to bring Good News to the poor. He has sent me to proclaim that captives will be released, that the blind will see, that the oppressed will be set free, and that the time of the Lord's favor has come.' He rolled up the scroll, handed it back to the attendant, and sat down. All eyes in the synagogue looked at him intently"—(Luke 4:17-20).

The passage Jesus read from speaks of the Messiah and His mission. If you turn to Isaiah and read the passage Jesus selected, the half of the sentence He left out is revealing. "The Spirit of the Sovereign Lord is upon me, for the Lord has anointed me to bring good news to the poor. He has sent me to comfort the brokenhearted and to proclaim that captives will be released and prisoners will be freed. He has sent me to tell those who mourn that the time of the Lord's favor has come…" Jesus stopped right there, mid-sentence. But the rest reads, "and with it, the day of God's anger against their enemies"—(Isaiah 61:1-2).

Though Isaiah saw the Messiah as doing this, Jesus stopped short because that was not the mission of the Messiah. Isaiah had revelation, but it wasn't 20/20 vision. That's because revelation is progressive and did not reach its fullness until Jesus came to reveal the Father. This is the reason people missed Jesus' mission the first time He came to earth. They were looking for a Messiah who would raise an army and destroy the Romans. They didn't get that Jesus was going to allow the Romans to destroy Him!

Even when Mary, Jesus' mother, sang her great song of praise, she totally missed it. "Oh, how my soul praises the Lord. How my spirit rejoices in God my Savior! For he took notice of his lowly servant girl, and from now on all generations will call me blessed. For the Mighty One is holy, and he has done great things for me. He shows mercy from generation to generation to all who fear him. His mighty arm has done tremendous things! He has scattered the proud and haughty ones. He has brought down princes from their thrones and exalted the humble. He has filled the hungry with good things and sent the rich away with empty hands"—(Luke 1:46-53). Her last two sentences reflect Israel's hopes that the Messiah will defeat the Romans. When we read the Scriptures, we want to make sure we don't force those kinds of handcuffs on Scripture or we will miss the very heart of what it is trying to tell us.

Scripture Is Inerrant, Infallible and Inspired

Does that then mean we cannot trust Scripture? God forbid! No! Scripture is infallible, inerrant and inspired. It is inspired in that God moved those men to write under His guidance. It is inerrant in that it says what God wanted it to say. His desire was to meet the people where they were at that time in their understanding of Him, and progressively move them forward. And it is infallible in that it accomplishes exactly what God intends it to accomplish, which is to lead us to Jesus.

Jesus joined two disciples who were walking to the village of Emmaus. He had just risen from the dead, but they did not recognize Him. They were commiserating His death, not knowing they were talking to Him. He gently reprimanded them for their lack of understanding about the Messiah. "Wasn't it clearly predicted that the Messiah would have to suffer all these things before entering his glory," Jesus asked (Luke 24:26). Then Luke tells us Jesus began with the writings of Moses (which is Genesis through Deuteronomy) and walked them through all the Scriptures, showing them how they were all written to point to Him. Wouldn't you love to have been in that Bible study! According to Jesus, every bit of the Old Testament pointed to Him.

The Apostle Paul said of the Law, "Therefore the Law has become our tutor to lead us to Christ, so that we may be justified by faith" (Galatians 3:24). Mark Moore shares that we have often made the mistake of placing the Scriptures above Jesus, and in so doing, have missed the point. "Jesus is the object of our faith and he is our understanding of God. This means that we are better served by interpreting our Bibles right to left. We begin with Jesus, as the object of our faith, and then allow the object of our faith to provide clarity to the hazy shadows of the Old Testament. Rather than sorting out how Jesus fits into our already formed understanding of God, we must allow Jesus to reveal God's true nature and character to us."[7] Jesus is exactly like God and God is exactly like Jesus. And when there seems to be a contradiction in the Biblical record we must interpret it through the lens of Jesus. For Jesus is the full and complete revelation of the Father.

The Goal of Discipleship Is to Be Like God

All of this has some incredible implications for us. As disciples we want to be like God. Paul instructed us, "Imitate God, therefore, in everything you do, because you are his dear children" (Ephesians 5:1). If we have a clouded image of God, however, it can distort our idea of what we are to become. In fact, we become like the god we serve. "And those who make idols are just like them, as are all who trust in them" (Psalm 115:8). Those who see God as judgmental and hate-filled become like that "god".

That's the interpretation of God we get from groups like the Westboro Baptist church. When Michael Jackson died in 2009, they announced plans to picket his funeral and stated on their website, "We will be there to tell you to thank God for the death of this filthy, adulterous, idolatrous, gender-confused, nationality-confused, unthankful brute beast." As part of their protest, they released a song titled *God Hates the World*, a takeoff of Jackson's charity hit *We Are the World*.[8] That doesn't square with Scripture that clearly states, "For this is how God loved the world: He gave His one and only Son, so that everyone who believes in Him will not perish but have eternal life" (John 3:16). This is a group that translates the Bible from left to right; filtering their understanding of God through the judgmental portions of the text. Every understanding of God is interpreted through that lens.

A California pastor made headlines when he posted his sermon, celebrating the death of 49 people at a gay nightclub in Florida. The sermon has been removed from the site, but in his sermon he said, "The tragedy is that more of them didn't die. I'm kind of upset he didn't finish the job — because these people are predators."[9]

That kind of hate speech doesn't represent God. But if you were to take a strict Old Testament interpretation, you would have to say they were accurate. Leviticus says that gays need to be executed (Leviticus 20:13). But that's not the heart of Jesus. He loved everyone, no matter what sin they committed. I don't think Jesus would have gone into that Florida bar and shot those gay people. He would have gone into that bar and showed them the way to life. Jesus was criticized precisely because He showed kindness to those living outside the accepted religious norms. "Later, Matthew invited Jesus and his disciples to his home as dinner guests, along with many tax collectors and other disreputable sinners. But when the Pharisees saw this, they asked his disciples, "Why does your teacher eat with such scum?" When Jesus heard this, he said, "Healthy people don't need a doctor—sick people do." Then he added, "Now go and learn the meaning of this Scripture: 'I want you to show mercy, not offer sacrifices.' For I have come to call not those who think they are righteous, but those who know they are sinners" (Matthew 9:10-13). When Jesus mentioned sacrifices, He was referring to religious rituals. The Pharisees were adept at keeping the rules. They knew all the codes and how to conduct themselves. Jesus said the heart attitudes of mercy and compassion are far more important than religious rituals. With Jesus, people were more important than rules.

Jesus Defines Holiness Differently Than We Have Traditionally Thought

Our understanding of God must come from Jesus. We need to be like Him for God is like Jesus. Earlier when we read the verse where Paul admonished us to be imitators of God, we stopped too soon. He goes on to further define what he meant. "Imitate God, therefore, in everything you do, because you are his dear children. **Live a life filled with love, following the example of Christ**. He loved us and offered himself as a sacrifice for us, a pleasing aroma to God" (Ephesians 5:1-2 emphasis added).

In our quest for discipleship, we want to be holy (Matthew 5:48; 1 Peter 1:16). But again, if we are going to shoot for holiness or "perfection" (a word Jesus used), our focus must be on Jesus, for God is like Him. When we think of holiness, if we take our cues from the Old Testament instead of Jesus, we can become legalistic. We may not be hate-filled like the Westboro Baptists, but we can become stern and judgmental. Consequently, holiness becomes about rules and restrictions. It becomes more about what you don't do, rather than who you are.

My wife and I were visiting our son and his wife in Seattle where they live. I am addicted to coffee and am a huge Starbucks fan. So of course, when in Seattle, we had to go to the original store in the Market Place. It is a favorite tourist attraction, and as such, the line stretched outside, down the street. There was a musical group set up on the sidewalk, playing and singing for the tourists. I filmed a portion of one of their numbers and posted it on Facebook. True to form, some legalistic pastor saw my post and felt it was his sacred duty to set me straight. He scolded me for supporting such a wicked company. He asked me how I could consider myself a man of God and patronize a company that openly supports the LGBT community. For him, holiness was about pointing the finger at others and charging them for not adhering to a strict code of conduct (a code, by the way, that they create).

Because he scolded me publically, I responded back. If we were to boycott every company that supported causes we don't agree with, we wouldn't be able to buy groceries, deposit money in a bank or fill our cars with gas. Jesus said to be in the world, but not of it. Paul wrote to the Corinthian church, "When I wrote to you before, I told you not to associate with people who indulge in sexual sin. But I wasn't talking about unbelievers who indulge in sexual sin, or are greedy, or cheat people, or worship idols. You would have to leave this world to avoid people like that. I meant that you are not to associate with anyone who claims to be a believer yet indulges in sexual sin, or is greedy, or worships idols, or is abusive, or is a drunkard, or cheats people" (1 Corinthians 5:9-11). Paul's problem was with the hypocrite; one who focuses on the splinters in someone else's eye, but ignores the giant beam sticking out of their own head.

Just a few weeks prior to visiting the Seattle Starbucks, I was in Rochester, New York. I stopped into a Starbucks in the downtown area. A homeless man looking for a meal approached me as I was sitting down to enjoy my coffee. I agreed to buy him some food, but invited him to sit with me. We had a conversation over a breakfast sandwich and coffee. During our meal he shared his heart with me, and I was privileged to pray with him. He committed his life to Christ—right there in the lion's den. And you know what? Jesus was right there.

And had He been physically present, I have no doubt He would have been sipping on a Grande Redeye right along with us.

When Jesus came to earth, the Jews were looking for a conqueror to overthrow Rome. They wanted a mighty warrior. We do too. We want a God who takes no prisoners. When Jesus sets up His kingdom we want Him to kick some Satanic butt. But wait a minute; Jesus has already set up His kingdom. "One day the Pharisees asked Jesus, 'When will the Kingdom of God come?' Jesus replied, 'The Kingdom of God can't be detected by visible signs. You won't be able to say, 'Here it is!' or 'It's over there!' For the Kingdom of God is already among you'" (Luke 17:20-21).

We might think Jesus' kingdom doesn't look very kingly. Look how He was born; in a cave used as an animal stall. He came in the vulnerability of an infant and was rushed away to Egypt in the middle of the night to escape the powerful Herod. He was weak and subject to pain. When arrested, He rebuked Peter for wielding a dagger and commanded him to put it away. Jesus wouldn't make a good action hero.

The former mega-church pastor, Mark Driscoll once said in a sermon, "I cannot worship a guy I can beat up."[10] But that's just it; we did beat Him up. We flogged Him and nailed Him to a cross. Jesus' view of authority and power was completely different than ours. "But Jesus called them together and said, 'You know that the rulers in this world lord it over their people, and officials flaunt their authority over those under them. But among you it will be different. Whoever wants to be a leader among you must be your servant, and whoever wants to be first among you must become your slave. For even the Son of Man came not to be served but to serve others and to give his life as a ransom for many'" (Matthew 20:25-28). Reigning through weakness, serving through love—that is what Jesus is all about. And it is what the Father is all about as well.

But we may think, *Now wait a minute. God the Father will destroy His enemies. He will place them under His feet like a footstool.* Yes, but how? By allowing the serpent to strike His heal; by being nailed to a cross. It is through His defeat that grace wins. And He is saying that is how we are to live.

Discipleship is about holiness, and holiness is about being like Jesus. Let's bring that right down to where we live. As Americans we want our rights. But Jesus says to lay them down. The Apostle Paul addressed some church people who were being cheated by other Christians. Their private space was violated. It was their right to demand justice. But Paul challenged them with the way of *agape*. "Even to have such lawsuits with one another is a defeat for you. Why not just accept the injustice and leave it at that? Why not let yourselves be cheated" (1 Corinthians 7:7). Is he kidding? He can't really mean that, can He?

Jesus said we are to be perfect as the Father is perfect. But He didn't mean we were to execute a flawless moral performance. He said those words in the context of relationships. "You have heard the law that says, 'Love your neighbor' and hate your enemy. But I say, love your enemies! Pray for those who persecute you! In that way, you will be acting as true children of your Father in heaven. For he gives his sunlight to both the evil and the good, and he sends rain on the just and the unjust alike. If you love only those who love you, what reward is there for that? Even corrupt tax collectors do that much. If you are kind only to your friends, how are you different from anyone else? Even pagans do that. But you are to be perfect, even as your Father in heaven is perfect" (Matthew 5:43-48).

Discipleship isn't about rules, regulations and spiritual disciplines. It's about love. It's about relationships. We are to be like God and God is exactly like Jesus. That sets the course for our discipleship journey.

3
The Christmas Dance

An Invitation To the Dance

Christmas is America's biggest holiday. I am sure you have noticed we begin celebrating earlier every year. I had to run into Lowes before Halloween this year. When I entered the store there were goblins, ghosts and witches, displayed next to Christmas trees. I don't doubt that eventually we will see trees displayed during the 4th of July weekend. I get it. We love the decorations, lights, music, family, food, and the gifts. Christmas is king. It is also one of the busiest times in the life of the church. Christmas parties, musicals, Bethlehem drive-thrus and pageants fill the calendar.

Theologically, however, Christmas takes a back seat to Easter. The death and resurrection of Jesus are the big events in the Christian calendar. The "bells and whistles" of Christmas are huge, but the birth of Jesus is seen as a warm up to the real drama. We think the incarnation was necessary so Jesus could die. Other than that, we give it little theological importance. As a result, the meaning of Christmas is relegated to slogans on Christmas cards—"Peace on earth", mangers and angels. And then, there's the many gifts. In fact, one year I received a Christmas card that proudly displayed the verse, "And those who dwell on the earth will rejoice over them and celebrate; and they will send gifts to one another" (Revelation 11:10). Sounds nice, but somebody in the card department didn't do their homework. That verse describes the satanic beast killing God's two prophets. The people of the earth are so overjoyed the prophets are dead, they leave their bodies to rot in the streets for three days and send gifts to one another in celebration.

The truth is, the night Jesus was born is one of the most glorious, mysterious events in all of human history. John Clark quotes J. I. Packer, "The Christmas event of Christ's birth is where 'the profoundest and most unfathomable depths of the Christian revelation lie . . .' Nothing in fiction is so fantastic as is this truth of the Incarnation."[11] The incarnation is when God became man, but it's much, much more than that. "So the Word became human and made his home among us" (John 1:14). "As he considered this, an angel of the Lord appeared to him in a dream. 'Joseph, son of David,' the angel said, 'do not be afraid to take Mary as your wife. For the child within her was conceived by the Holy Spirit. And she will have a son, and you are to name him Jesus, for he will save his people from their sins.' All of this occurred to fulfill the Lord's message through his prophet: 'Look! The virgin will conceive a child! She will give birth to a son, and they will call him Immanuel, which means God is with us' " (Matthew 1:20-23).

When Jesus was born God became a man—completely divine, and completely human. Jesus is one person, but He possesses two natures: a perfect divine nature and a perfect human nature. His human nature is exactly like ours. His divine nature is exactly like the Father's and the Holy Spirit's. They are perfectly joined together into one person. My words here are very intentional. The two natures are joined together, they are not mixed; like mixing two ingredients that form another substance. Jesus did not join human and divine to form a new type of being. Think of it this way, if you mix blue and yellow paint you get green paint. It is no longer yellow. It is no longer blue. It is now something new; it is green. That is not how we understand Jesus Christ. The two natures are not mixed to form some kind of unique super nature. The two natures are joined together into one Person: fully divine and fully human. His human nature is not somehow changed to be something different than ours. He is just like us. And His divine nature is not changed into something less than God. He is just as divine as the Father.

Jesus becomes a bridge between God and man

We may not spend much time thinking about such things, but if we roll that out, it has world-shaking implications. It means Jesus became a bridge between God and man (1 Timothy 2:5). Jesus is exactly as God is, and He is exactly as we are. That means through Jesus, God and mankind are united. He has joined Himself to our humanity. Jesus came to reveal God to us (Colossians 1:15). But that means far more than simply showing us what God is like. If that were the entire purpose of His mission, He could have just written it down. His purpose was not limited to explaining what God is like. As a bridge, fully divine and fully human, His mission is to share the life of God with us. In Jesus Christ, divine and human are joined so when we are joined to Christ, we are brought into union with God. "When I am raised to life again, you will know that I am in my Father, and you are in me, and I am in you" (John 14:20). Jesus makes it possible for us to know God on an experiential level. We don't just know about Him, but we know Him relationally. That is what the Bible calls eternal life. "And this is the way to have eternal life—to know you, the only true God, and Jesus Christ, the one you sent to earth" (John 17:3). We are invited into a relationship that is mind-blowing. God invites us into the private chambers of His inner heart where Father, Son and Holy Spirit commune.

God the Father, God the Son and God the Holy Spirit are three distinct persons, yet they are One God. They dwell in one another, not just with one another. John Clark says it this way, "Their individual characteristics instead of dividing them from one another unite them indivisibly together, the Father in the Son and the Spirit, the Son in the Father and the Spirit, and the Spirit in the Father and the Son. The Father is not Father apart from the Son and the Spirit, the Son is not the Son apart from the Father and the Spirit, and the Spirit is not the Spirit apart from the Father and the Son, for each is who he is in his wholeness as true God of true God in the wholeness of the other two who are each true God of true God."[12] The church father, John of Damascus wrote, "Such is the fellowship in the Godhead that the Father and the Son not only embrace each other, but they also enter into each other, permeate each other, and dwell in each other. One in being, they are also always one in the intimacy of their friendship."[13]

That sounds a little complicated, I know, but let me offer a word picture from Jonathan Marlow that may help clarify the concept. "The theologians in the early church tried to describe this wonderful reality that we call Trinity. If any of you have ever been to a Greek wedding, you may have seen their distinctive way of dancing. It's called perichoresis. There are not two dancers, but at least three. They start to go in circles, weaving in and out in this very beautiful pattern of motion. They start to go faster and faster and faster, all the while staying in perfect rhythm and in sync with each other. Eventually, they are dancing so quickly (yet so effortlessly) that as you look at them, it just becomes a blur. Their individual identities are part of a larger dance. The early church fathers and mothers looked at that dance and said, 'That's what the Trinity is like.' It's a harmonious set of relationships in which there is mutual giving and receiving. The Father, the Son, and the Holy Spirit have been in a state of all-consuming but ever-generating love for each other from before all time. The perichoresis is the dance of love."[14]

Eternal Life Is Not Something Jesus Gives Us
Eternal Life Is Sharing In the Life of the Eternal, Triune God

Jesus came to this world so He could unite with humanity and pull us into the Divine Dance. We are called into the relationship of the Trinity when we are united to Christ. Saint Peter described it this way: "For by these He has granted to us His precious and magnificent promises, so that by them you may become **partakers of the divine nature**" (2 Peter 1:4a emphasis added). We get to join in the dance! That's what Christmas is all about. It's an invitation to the dance. This affects our understanding of what eternal life is. Some people think eternal life means that God has changed His opinion about us because of what Jesus did on the cross. Or, they think eternal life is a reward Jesus gives us for believing in Him. Eternal life is far more than that. In Christ, God allows us to share in the very life enjoyed by the Father, the Son and the Holy Spirit.

Marcus Peter Johnson writes, "The eternal life he comes to give is nothing other than the life and love he eternally shares with the Father and the Spirit; he has brought that life into our humanity that we might share in it. It is eternal life because it is a sharing in the life of all life, the life that generates and sustains all things. This life is available to us only in the incarnate Son of God."[15] This is a reiteration of what the Apostle John wrote, "And we know that the Son of God has come, and he has given us understanding so that we can know the true God.

And now we live in fellowship with the true God because we live in fellowship with his Son, Jesus Christ. He is the only true God, and he is eternal life" (1 John 5:20).

How Do We Join the Dance?

It's one thing to know it, but how do we experience it? How do we join the dance? This is part of the Holy Spirit's role. Please do not think the Holy Spirit is a replacement for Jesus—that somehow He is here with us while Jesus and the Father are in heaven. When we relegate the Holy Spirit to the role of a surrogate God, He becomes nothing more than a spiritual tool to manipulate. He becomes the force by which we express the gifts of the Spirit. But don't do it. The Holy Spirit's role is far more than that. His role is to bind us together with the Godhead. He doesn't replace the Father and the Son; He introduces us to them. He ushers us into the dance.

Jesus brought the divine dance into human experience when He became a man. When the Holy Spirit joins us to Jesus, we share in the same dance as Jesus. Picture the dance as a moving circle of motion, like the parameter of a hurricane. You have most likely seen the pictures on a weather map of a moving hurricane. It forms a circular pinwheel that rotates clockwise as the storm approaches the coast. The high velocity winds beat against the shore until the eye of the storm moves over the land. The eye is the center, and is unusually calm. But then the backside of the storm hits and is more ferocious than the front side. Within the eye, however, there is an atmosphere, an eerie stillness. The eye feels safe, but dangerous all at the same time. The eye of the hurricane is like the terrible, but wonderful dance of God. There is an atmosphere within the circle, both wonderful and terrifying. Within the circle is an exchange between the Persons of the Trinity. I believe that atmosphere is the fruit of the Spirit: love, joy, peace, patience, kindness, goodness, gentleness, faithfulness, self-control. All those characteristics are shared between Father, Son and Holy Spirit. If one could stand in the middle of that holy storm, the predominate emotion within that divine atmosphere would be joy. Richard J. Vincent comments "joy is the passionate overflow of delight and desire between

Father, Son, and Spirit." Jurgen Schultz says, "The Triune God lives in an incomparable celebration of eternal joy."[16]

Jesus wants us to experience that joy. "I have told you these things so that you will be filled with my joy. Yes, your joy will overflow" (John 15:11). Our experience of Jesus' joy was a major factor in His mission and His great prayer to the Father. "Now I am coming to you. I told them many things while I was with them in this world so they would be filled with my joy"(John 17:13). Jesus wants to bring us into the dance so we experience the same joy He does. As partakers of the divine nature, God's joy becomes ours. And that joy is not tied to painful circumstances. It comes from an awareness that God surrounds us in the divine dance, so that even when life is filled with pain, we are not removed from the circle.

A relationship with God isn't about performance, where we try to keep the laws of God. It's not about legal transactions, where we seek forgiveness as a ticket to heaven. A relationship with God is participatory, where we join the dance through the Holy Spirit and participate in the life of God that is shared within the Trinity. Jesus came into this world to make that life available to us. When we lose sight of that, we relegate Christianity to a mere religion: a lifeless requirement of duties to try and please a holy God. But Christ came that we might have life, and that we might have it more abundantly (John 10:10). He came so that we can enter into the divine dance and experience the life He shares with the Father and the Holy Spirit, and offers to us.

The Dance Comes to Earth

Through the Holy Spirit we are joined to Christ. As a result, we are invited into the dance. But there are two sides to this coin. Not only are we in Christ, but also Christ is in us. That's incredibly significant because being in Christ ushers us into His world, but even more amazing, Christ in us ushers Him into our world. Notice how Jesus described this inter connection. "When I am raised to life again, you will know that I am in my Father, and **you are in me and I am in you**" (John 14:20 emphasis added). That's not just poetic writing. Jesus is speaking of a reality that can change our lives.

We see this mentioned often in Scripture, and I suspect, we read right past it without really considering what it means. For example "For God wanted them to know that the riches and glory of Christ are for you Gentiles, too. And this is the secret: **Christ lives in you**. This gives you assurance of sharing his glory" (Colossians 1:27 emphasis added).

Christ in us assures us of the hope of glory. We often think of glory as referring to heaven, but the word means worship or praise. It means that our lives will be a living praise to God. Paul expressed the same idea in Ephesians. "All praise to God, the Father of our Lord Jesus Christ, who has blessed us with every spiritual blessing in the heavenly realms because **we are united with Christ**. Even before he made the world, God loved us and chose us in Christ to be holy and without fault in his eyes. God decided in advance to adopt us into his own family by **bringing us to himself through Jesus Christ**. This is what he wanted to do, and it gave him great pleasure. So we praise God for the glorious grace he has poured out on us who belong to his dear Son. He is so rich in kindness and grace that he purchased our freedom with the blood of his Son and forgave our sins. He has showered his kindness on us, along with all wisdom and understanding. God has now revealed to us his mysterious plan regarding Christ, a plan to fulfill his own good pleasure. And this is the plan: At the right time he will bring everything together under the authority of Christ—everything in heaven and on earth. Furthermore, **because we are united with Christ**, we have received an inheritance from God, for he chose us in advance, and he makes everything work out according to his plan. God's purpose was that we Jews who were the first to trust in Christ **would bring praise and glory to God**. And now you Gentiles have also heard the truth, the Good News that God saves you. And when you believed in Christ, **he identified you as his own by giving you the Holy Spirit**, whom he promised long ago. The Spirit is God's guarantee that he will give us the inheritance he promised and that he has purchased us to be his own people. He did this so **we would praise and glorify him**" (Ephesians 1:3-14 emphasis added). That's Christ in you the hope of glory.

The Vicarious Humanity of Christ

Paul states this idea the clearest in Galatians. "My old self has been crucified with Christ. It is no longer I who live, but **Christ lives in me**. So I live in this earthly body by trusting in the Son of God, who loved me and gave himself for me" (Galatians 2:20 emphasis added). Christ living His life in us introduces us to what is known as the vicarious humanity of Christ. Let me explain it this way; the word vicarious means someone who steps into our place and does what we can't do. We are familiar, perhaps with the vicarious death of Christ; that Christ died in our place. His death becomes our death. His resurrection becomes our resurrection. That means we reap the benefits of Jesus' death and resurrection when we are united to Him. His death makes it unnecessary for us to pay the price of death, and His resurrection guarantees our resurrection. He stood in our place and died for us and rose from the dead for us. We get that. But we overlook His vicarious life. Jesus not only died for us, but He lived for us. His life becomes our life.

Dr. G. Hunsinger in his book, *The Dimension of Depth: Thomas F. Torrance on the Sacraments,* states —"vicarious humanity means that everything Christ has done for us in his humanity was done in our place and on our behalf."[17] Caleb Smith adds, "From the beginning to the end, from Christmas to Easter, every moment of Jesus' life was something He did to save us. It didn't just start when He was led to the Cross. What Jesus was doing as a human being to save us started when the virgin conceived, and it's still going."[18]

Think of it this way: The people who wrote the Scriptures did so under the inspiration of the Holy Spirit. "All Scripture is inspired by God and profitable for teaching, for reproof, for correction, for training in righteousness" (2 Timothy 3:16). The word inspired means "God breathed." God moved upon the writers to put into words the things He wanted said. This wasn't automatic writing, like Edgar Cayce, who went into a trance, acting as a channel for a spirit, writing words without his knowledge or consent.[19] Instead, God moved upon the writers, but used their intellect, emotions, writing styles, skills and historical backgrounds. He was working through the filter of their personhood. They were fully conscious and aware of what they were doing, but also aware that God was working through them as they wrote. In the same way they practiced inspired writing, God wants us to practice inspired living. Christ wants to live through us, while filtering His life though our unique personhood.

God becoming a man reveals a most incredible reality. Jesus does not want us to try and copy His life. Instead, Jesus wants to live His life through us. That's what it means to be united with Christ. Through the agency of the Holy Spirit, He lives His life through us. Christian author, Bill Gillham helped me understand this years ago. He said Christians often live their lives like we use our cordless devices. We plug them in to charge them, and then run them down until they need another charge.[20] Christians sometimes think they're supposed to go to church (wrong—they are the church) and get recharged, and then step out into the next week to live for Jesus. Once their spiritual battery is drained, they need to come in again for a recharge. That is living according to the flesh and will produce failure. Christ wants us to stay plugged into Him moment by moment so He can live His life through us.

That is what John 15:4-5 is all about. "Remain in me, and I will remain in you. For a branch cannot produce fruit if it is severed from the vine, and you cannot be fruitful unless you remain in me. Yes, I am the vine; you are the branches. Those who remain in me, and I in them, will produce much fruit. For apart from me you can do nothing." Gillman writes, "Somehow the Deceiver has convinced us that we're to "live our lives for Jesus" (as if He were so impotent that He needed our help), instead of allowing Jesus Christ to express His own life through His own body—the individual members of His corporate church."[21]

Jesus Wants To Live His Life Through Us

Every part of Jesus' life was lived on our behalf. For example, let's think about repentance. When Jesus was baptized John didn't want to do it. "Then Jesus went from Galilee to the Jordan River to be baptized by John. But John tried to talk him out of it. 'I am the one who needs to be baptized by you,' he said, 'so why are you coming to me'" (Matthew 3:13-14). John had an issue with this because his was a baptism of repentance for sins (Acts 19:4). He was baptizing people who were guilty of sin and wanted to get right with God. Jesus didn't need to do that, so John didn't feel right in baptizing Him. But Jesus insisted. He said it was to fulfill all righteousness (Matthew 3:15).

Jesus repented for sins—not His own, but ours. When we were united with Jesus in salvation, His repentance became our repentance. When we repent from sin do we think we do it perfectly? Here is what perfect repentance looks like. "Just see what this godly sorrow produced in you! Such earnestness, such concern to clear yourselves, such indignation, such alarm, such longing to see me, such zeal, and such a readiness to punish wrong. You showed that you have done everything necessary to make things right" (2 Corinthians 7:11). I wonder how many of us get it right? What if we miss a sin? What if we don't say the right words, or have the right attitude? But if Christ is our life, then His repentance becomes ours. When we repent, even if ours is not perfect, His is. We don't have to be afraid we didn't do it right, because He did it right on our behalf. That's why Romans 8 says "there is no condemnation for those who belong to Christ Jesus" (Romans 8:1). Does that mean we don't need to repent? No, but we join our repentance to His.

Let's look at another example—our faith. Often we struggle because our faith seems weak. We wonder, if my faith is weak, will God answer my prayers? If I can't believe the right way, maybe things won't work out. No wonder nothing ever goes right; my faith is too small. But if Christ is our life, then His faith becomes our faith. I want to look at a verse that is so powerful but sadly, we have missed its full impact because of a wrong translation. "My old self has been crucified with Christ. It is no longer I who live, but Christ lives in me. So I live in this earthly body by trusting in the Son of God, who loved me and gave himself for me" (Galatians 2:20). Notice the phrase, "I live in this earthly body by trusting in the Son of God." Instead, many versions say, "I live by faith in the Son of God."

But this is one of those places where the King James Version got it right and it should not have been changed. Here's how the KJV words it, "I am crucified with Christ: nevertheless I live; yet not I, but Christ liveth in me: and the life which I now live in the flesh I live by the faith of the Son of God, who loved me, and gave himself for me" (Galatians 2:20 KJV). Did you catch it? The KJV says, "I live **by the faith of** the Son of God" (emphasis added). There's a very big difference between saying, "I live **by faith in** the Son of God," and saying, "I live **by the faith of** the Son of God." The modern translations are speaking of something we have toward Jesus; we have faith in Him. The KJV is speaking of something Jesus has for us; He has faith that He gives us. Do you see the difference? One is our faith toward Him; it's what we bring to the table. The other is His faith given to us; it's what He brings to the table.

Interestingly, many scholars are moving back to the KJV translation. The reason is because the Greek grammar allows the translation to be either way. The words "of"; as in, "faith of the son of God" and "in"; as in, "faith in the son of God," are not actually in the original Greek. So the interpretation has been left to whether the translator interpreted the phrase as a subjective genitive or an objective genitive, which is Greek talk and makes no sense to us. It all boils down to the context. Translators have to make a judgment call based on the context of the verse. Look again at Galatians 2:20. "I am crucified with Christ: nevertheless I live; **yet not I, but Christ liveth in me**: and the life which I now live in the flesh I live by the faith of the Son of God, who loved me, and gave himself for me" (emphasis added). Paul is writing about Jesus living within and through him (by the Holy Spirit); "yet not I but Christ lives in me." He is saying that Jesus is living His life through Paul. So it would be illogical to say it is done by Paul's own faith. One theological journal put it this way; "It makes much more sense contextually for him to mean that Christ's faith operates within him as Christ lives His life within him."[22]

That means faith is a gift from Christ. He lives His life in us and exercises His faith through us. Some might wonder how Jesus could have faith. He's God. He doesn't need faith. It is true He is God, but He also didn't need to repent. He did it for us. Notice when Jesus came out of the waters of baptism the Holy Spirit landed on Him. Then after His temptation in the wilderness, He went in the power of the

Holy Spirit (Luke 4:13-14). That was because He would minister as a man, in the power of the Spirit and operate by faith. But He did it for our sakes. That was part of the emptying Paul wrote about in Philippians. "You must have the same attitude that Christ Jesus had. Though he was God, he did not think of equality with God as something to cling to. Instead, **he gave up his divine privileges**; he took the humble position of a slave and was born as a human being" (Philippians 2:5-7 emphasis added).

That's why Jesus said greater works will we do because He goes to the Father. "I tell you the truth, anyone who believes in me will do the same works I have done, and **even greater works, because I am going to be with the Father**. You can ask for anything in my name, and I will do it, so that the Son can bring glory to the Father. Yes, ask me for anything in my name, and I will do it! If you love me, obey my commandments. And I will ask the Father, and he will give you another Advocate, who will never leave you. He is the Holy Spirit, who leads into all truth. The world cannot receive him, because it isn't looking for him and doesn't recognize him. But you know him, because **he lives with you now and later will be in you**. No, **I will not abandon you as orphans—I will come to you**" (John 14:12-18 emphasis added). That means He will supply the same Spirit-anointing He enjoyed.

All that Jesus did was done in faith. We are to operate by allowing His faith to work through us. Does that mean we don't need to have faith? Of course not. Dr. Baxter Kruger explains this by telling the story of two men who were on an icy river. One man was walking across when he heard a deep crack. He was in the middle of the river, so he got down on the ice and spread his limbs out to distribute his weight. He carefully crawled across until finally he reached the shore. About that time he heard a roaring thunder, and looked back to see a man with a team of horses ride out across the frozen river. The team raced across and the driver waved and smiled as he led the horses up the bank onto land. They both had different levels of faith. One had little faith, and the other had so much faith that he drove his horses on the ice. But it didn't really matter what level of faith each had, because the ice held both of them. The thing that was important wasn't their level of faith, but the quality of the ice. And so it is with our faith. It may be small or great, but what matters is Christ. He holds us, whether our faith is weak or strong.

When Peter walked on the water he looked at the waves and began to sink because his faith started to fail. Immediately Jesus reached out and grabbed Peter's hand, demonstrating that where Peter's faith was weak, Jesus made up the difference. It's a picture of our faith working together. We trust in His faith, but we also exercise our faith, and where ours lacks, He makes up the difference. It's not that Jesus believes 100% and we don't need to believe at all. Nor is it that we believe 50% and He believes 50%, because then we are back to trusting in our faith. No, Christ believes 100% and we believe 100%, but what we do, we do through the agency of Christ who is in us.[23]

He was born to live a perfect human life, and His life becomes our life so that when we are united to Him through the Holy Spirit, He can live His life through us. The implications of that are gigantic as Professor T. F. Torrance shares. "Jesus believes when I am unable to believe. Jesus acts when I am unable to act. Jesus loves when I am unable to love. Jesus forgives when I am unable to forgive. Jesus lives when I am dead in my sins. That is the power of truth become personal, the power of a vicarious life."[24]

Learning How to Dance

It is wonderful that Jesus invites us to the dance and that He brings the dance to us, but how do we experience that reality in our lives? It doesn't just automatically happen. Otherwise, we wouldn't need to talk about it, because we would all be living it. We are to rest in Christ and allow Him to live through us. Human effort ceases, but there is still something we have to do to get into that state of rest. Hebrews says, "So there is a special rest still waiting for the people of God. For all who have entered into God's rest have rested from their labors, just as God did after creating the world. So let us do our best to enter that rest" (Hebrews 4:9-11). The New Living Translation says we are to do our best to enter that rest. I like the New American Standard Bible here because it says, "let us be diligent to enter that rest." We have to work at resting. So how do we do that? In the following chapters we will unpack this in specific detail, but I want to lay out some general steps we need to take in order to "enter that rest."

First, we have to take hold of eternal life. That sounds like a cliché, but trust me, it is not. I think we may have some wrong ideas about what eternal life is. Some equate it with extended, never ending existence. It can be dumbed down to a ticket to heaven so we can live forever. But unending existence is just a byproduct. That's like saying the reason we go fishing is to sit in a boat on the water and enjoy the gentle rocking of the waves. No, that's a byproduct, but the purpose is to catch fish.

Some people equate eternal life with a set of codes, laws or principles by which to live. We think eternal life has to do with being a good Christian. That is wrong as well. God doesn't want us to be "good Christians." If anything, He wants us to be dead Christians. (I'll explain what I mean by that in a moment). Eternal life is not a religion. It's not about being a Protestant, a Catholic or a Christian. All of those ideas are based on the premise that eternal life is something God gives us, or that it is tied to our spiritual beliefs. That's like trying to find a solution when we are asking the wrong question. Let's say we are trying to solve a math equation, but instead of asking how to solve the problem, we ask how to spell the word Algebra. We are altogether in the wrong place. The Apostle John introduces us to a completely different paradigm. He teaches us to think in all together different categories. "We proclaim to you the one who existed from the beginning, whom we have heard and seen. We saw him with our own eyes and touched him with our own hands. He is the Word of life. This one who is life itself was revealed to us, and we have seen him. And now we testify and proclaim to you that **he is the one who is eternal life**. He was with the Father, and then he was revealed to us" (1 John 1:1-2 emphasis added). Eternal life is not an object, a program, a religion or a thing that is given. Eternal life is a person. Eternal life is Jesus. In John 14:6, Jesus said, "I am the way, the truth, and the life." That is a crucial distinction, because in order to experience the life of Jesus lived through us, we have to first make sure that we have a relationship with a person, and not just a religion. Let me tease that out a little bit to help you see what I am getting at.

Some people, for example, have more of a relationship with the Scripture than they do with Jesus. They are more connected to the written word than they are the Living Word. I get it; the Bible is something we can touch and see. It speaks directly to us, while Jesus is invisible, inaudible and intangible. Christian blogger Mark Moore puts it this way, "The normative experience of early Christians was a relationship with Jesus. The normative experience of American Christians is a relationship with the Bible. The difference in these two experiences is HUGE! Christians in all times and all places are CHRIST-ians, not BIBLE-ians. Jesus is the object of our faith and he is our understanding of God. This means that we are better served by interpreting our Bibles right to left. We begin with Jesus, as the object of our faith, and then allow the object of our faith to provide clarity to the hazy shadows of the Old Testament. Rather than sorting out how Jesus fits into our already formed understanding of God, we must allow Jesus to reveal God's true nature and character to us. For BIBLE-ians this may sound blasphemous. Irreverent. Heretical. I completely understand. I was once a BIBLE-ian myself. But allow me to ask you a simple question: If you woke up tomorrow in the first century without a Bible, having never had one, what would you do? My guess is that you would pray more. Another way of putting it–you would spend more time encountering the actual living Jesus. You'd spend less time trying to sort out the meaning of obscure verses. You'd spend less time forming airtight theological constructs. You would wrestle with what you had–a story that centered on one dying for his enemies and inviting us to live the same life–the story of Jesus. This Jesus would shape your understanding of God and you would believe that God is love and that you were called to be like him. You would actually be a CHRIST-ian."[25]

I am not diminishing the importance of the Bible. I love studying the Bible, but the Bible is a tool God has given us to point us to Him. If we are more concerned with studying the Bible to gain knowledge, than to deepen our relationship with Jesus, then we may be guilty of Bibliolotry. If we hold to a literalist interpretation of the Bible, even when it contradicts the nature and character of Jesus, then we may be guilty of bibliloltry. If we spend more time studying passages of

Scripture than we do talking to Jesus, then we may be guilty of bibliolotry. If we are more in love with Scripture than we are with Jesus, then we are definitely guilty of bibliolotry.

I had to repent when first confronted with this idea. I had more of a relationship with the word than I did with Jesus. I studied about Him. I dissected the Greek and Hebrew. I diagramed the sentences and was careful about my hermeneutical approach to the Scriptures. I love studying the word, but there is a subtle danger in being drawn to the knowledge of the Scriptures, rather than getting to know the Living Word. I had to confess my idolatry and repent of Biblical intellectualism. It is so easy to be ever learning, but not come to an intimate knowledge of the One whom we are learning about. Are you in love with Jesus or His book?

When we look at eternal life as a reward we receive, then we can fall into another trap as well. Let me get in to it by asking you another question: do you serve God because you love Jesus, or because you fear going to hell? For generations evangelical Christianity has taught that there are two possible eternal destinies for man: heaven, or hell. I totally agree there is a heaven and there is a hell, but there are those from as far back as the first century who do not believe in an eternal torment in hell. Some of the church fathers and early theologians taught that if there is a hell it is restorative rather than punitive; meaning God uses hell to purge one of sin and restore them to a relationship with Him, rather than it simply being a place to punish the sinner for eternity. Athanasius and Gregory of Nazianzus, among others, promoted such ideas. Later theologians, such as John Stott and F.F. Bruce, also took a softer view of hell. C.S. Lewis said, "The doors of hell are locked from the inside."[26] I am not arguing for their point, but I raise it, because I want to use it to make another point. Is that as clear as mud?

The argument against hell is in the Christian conversation right now. In fact, it is in the evangelical conversation. What I am interested in, however, is the common push back that is raised when someone argues against an eternal, conscious torment. What I have heard people say, in defense of the doctrine of hell, is that if there is no hell, or if hell is only temporary, then no one would bother getting saved. There is no motivation to live for God, it is believed, if everyone will ultimately arrive in heaven. "Live the way you want," they say, "because you are going to go to heaven anyway." I just heard of a conversation the other day by someone who presented that defense. They said they would have no motivation to live for Jesus if they did not fear going to hell. Please pause for a moment to honestly think about your answer to that question. If there were no hell and you would automatically go to heaven, would you live for Jesus?

If your answer is probably not, then that reveals a serious problem. That answer reveals something about your heart. Do you believe because you want to avoid punishment, or do you love the Lord? If we serve God because of the fear of hell then at the very least we are serving from a motivation of law, which stirs up sin and makes growth impossible. In other words, the Law condemns because of sin, so to avoid condemnation we are choosing to live for God. But that is a motivation to try and comply with the Law so as to avoid hell. But when we live to satisfy the Law it stirs up sin. As a result, we live in spiritual defeat, even though we claim to be a Christian.

But that's not the worst thing. If we only serve God out of fear of going to hell, it can mean we are serving out of fear of punishment rather than love for Jesus. That means we are not really in love with Jesus. We are simply looking for a get out of hell free card. There is no relationship in that. It's dead religion. Before we can experience the life of Jesus living through us, we need to make sure we are in love with Jesus; that we have a personal relationship with a Person, and not just a theological, or emotional tie with a religion. We do not simply believe in an historical event that took place 2000 years ago. We are not following words written on the pages of the Bible. Rather, we are walking in a loving relationship with the Living Christ who is alive in us right now. That's the first thing we have to do in order to experience the divine dance. We must take hold of eternal life—we must be in love with the living Lord.

Objective vs. Subjective Reality

The second thing we have to do, is believe objective reality before we can experience subjective reality. In other words, there are certain things the Bible says are true. We have to believe them before we can experience them. It is important to realize that living the Christian life is nothing we have to achieve. Jesus has already done it for us. He lived the perfect life in our place. Thus, we live by letting Him live His life through us, but we have to believe that objective truth before we can experience it.

The Apostle Paul hints at this in his letter to the Colossian church. "For you died to this life, and your real life is hidden with Christ in God. And when Christ, who is your life, is revealed to the whole world, you will share in all his glory" (Colossians 3:3-4). Notice this verse says our real life is hidden with Christ in God. Hidden means it is not obvious. Our real life is in Christ, but it's not something we automatically see. We have to believe it first.

Scripture describes us as already attaining God's planned purposes for us. "For God knew his people in advance, and he chose them to become like his Son, so that his Son would be the firstborn among many brothers and sisters. And having chosen them, he called them to come to him. And having called them, he gave them right standing with himself. And having given them right standing, he gave them his glory" (Romans 8:29-30). This says God has already done these things; He has already chosen us, called us, justified and glorified us. I get the chosen, called and justified, but glorified? I didn't think that happened until we entered eternity. Paul put it all in the past tense, because every one of these things are true, because Christ is our life. "But by His doing you are in Christ Jesus, who became to us wisdom from God, and righteousness and sanctification, and redemption" (1 Corinthians 1:30 NASB). Because we believe that, we then can do the next two things.

Futility of Trusting In Self-Effort

It is imperative we stop trusting in our own efforts. In order for us to be saved, sin and death had to be destroyed. Who destroyed sin and death? The right answer is Jesus. How did He do it? By dying on the cross and rising from the dead. When did He do it? 2000 years ago. Were any of us born then? Did we have anything to do with it? The securing of our salvation through Jesus' death and resurrection was nothing we did. Jesus did it. We are just asked to believe it. "Jesus told them, 'This is the only work God wants from you: Believe in the one he has sent'" (John 6:29). Our job is to believe. But even our ability to believe is something God gives us. "God saved you by his grace when you believed. And you can't take credit for this; it is a gift from God. Salvation is not a reward for the good things we have done, so none of us can boast about it" (Ephesians 2:8-9). When we began this journey it was not by any human effort. Our ability, IQ, talent, strength, personality or pedigree did not save us.

Keeping that in mind, listen to the question the Apostle Paul asked the Galatian Christians. "This is the only thing I want to find out from you: did you receive the Spirit by the works of the Law, or by hearing with faith?" (Galatians 3:2). The right answer was faith. Then Paul asked a follow up question. "Are you so foolish? Having begun by the Spirit, are you now being perfected by the flesh?" (Galatians 3:3). God saved us by the Spirit working through our faith. And because Jesus, the Father and the Spirit are one, it was Jesus working through us. If that's how we began this journey, why would we think we can finish the journey in our own strength?

Human effort to accomplish God's purpose for our lives will end in failure. God had promised Abraham a son, but he was getting old and he and Sarah had not been able to conceive. In fact, she was beyond the normal child bearing age. But Sarah had a plan. God said Abraham would have a promised child, but He never said anything about Sarah. So she suggested to Abraham he sleep with her servant Hagar and provide them a child through her. I can't begin to think how awkward that conversation must have been. Abraham reluctantly accepted. At least, if he was smart, he acted reluctant. They tried to help God out with His plan, and as a result, Ishmael was born. If you know this family's history at all, you know the birth of Ishmael has produced nothing but trouble for thousands of years.

When Abraham was 100 and Sarah was 90, God allowed her to get pregnant—an outright miracle. When Isaac, the promised child was born, it was clear that even though Abraham and Sarah "went through the motions" that child was a miracle from God. God got all the credit for Isaac. When Abraham worked in the power of his own flesh, he produced an Ishmael. When Abraham walked by faith in the power of God, Isaac was born. So it is with us. When we work in the power of our flesh, all we produce is trouble. Even when we try to do good things—like live the Christian life—our self-effort produces failure. Paul outlines this in great detail in his letter to the Roman church.

"Well then, am I suggesting that the law of God is sinful? Of course not! In fact, it was the law that showed me my sin. I would never have known that coveting is wrong if the law had not said, "You must not covet." But sin used this command to arouse all kinds of covetous desires within me! If there were no law, sin would not have that power. At one time I lived without understanding the law. But when I learned the command not to covet, for instance, the power of sin came to life, and I died. So I discovered that the law's commands, which were supposed to bring life, brought spiritual death instead. Sin took advantage of those commands and deceived me; it used the commands to kill me. But still, the law itself is holy, and its commands are holy and right and good. But how can that be? Did the law, which is good, cause my death? Of course not! Sin used what was good to bring about my condemnation to death. So we can see how terrible sin really is. It uses God's good commands for its own evil purposes. So the trouble is not with the law, for it is spiritual and good. The trouble is with me, for I am all too human, a slave to sin. I don't really understand myself, for I want to do what is right, but I don't do it. Instead, I do what I hate. But if I know that what I am doing is wrong, this shows that I agree that the law is good. So I am not the one doing wrong; it is sin living in me that does it. And I know that nothing good lives in me, that is, in my sinful nature. I want to do what is right, but I can't. I want to do what is good, but I don't. I don't want to do what is wrong, but I do it anyway. But if I do what I don't want to do, I am not really the one doing wrong; it is sin living in me that does it. I have discovered this principle of life—that when I want to do what is right, I inevitably do what is wrong. I love God's law with all my heart. But there is another power within me that is at war with my mind. This power makes me a slave to the sin that is still within me. Oh, what a miserable person I am! Who will free me from this life that is dominated by sin and death? Thank God! The answer is in Jesus Christ our Lord. So you see how it is: In my mind I really want to obey God's law, but because of my sinful nature I am a slave to sin" (Romans 7:7-25).

As soon as we try to do what is right, we set ourselves up for failure, because human effort stirs up sin. Notice at the end of his paragraph Paul said the answer is Jesus. It's not us trying to live for Jesus, but it's allowing Jesus to live through us: inspired living. We live this life the way we started it, by faith in Jesus—allowing Him to express His life through us.

The Power of Abiding

Finally, if we are going to experience the life of Jesus expressed through us, we must live in abiding prayer. Jesus said, "Remain in me, and I will remain in you. For a branch cannot produce fruit if it is severed from the vine, and you cannot be fruitful unless you remain in me. Yes, I am the vine; you are the branches. Those who remain in me, and I in them, will produce much fruit. For apart from me you can do nothing" (John 15:4-5). The branch is the conduit through which the sap must flow, but it is the vine, not the branch, that produces the fruit. The fruit is the product of the vine. The vine uses the branch to deliver the sap and to display the fruit. Without the vine, the branch has no power to create the fruit. The fruit exists because of the vine. We are nothing without the vine. Our purpose is to allow the sap (the life of Jesus) to be displayed through our lives (i.e. the fruit of the Spirit). How does that work? It's simple, but it takes trust. When engaging in life, we know that Jesus is in us and with us and wants to act through us. By faith we invite Him to display Himself through us, and then trust that He will. I love the way Bill Gillham expressed this in his book, *What God Wishes Christians Knew About Christianity*. With his folksy style, he makes it easy to understand.

"The boss buzzed you on the intercom and told you to come to his office. He said that the report you had submitted for the quarter was unacceptable, and he gave you one week to rewrite it. That's the sort of hell on earth that Christ has saved you from. As you're sitting there with your heart in your throat, you're to think, Lord Jesus, I'm so glad that I don't have to do this rewrite. You are my life and this is Your baby. Thank You for saving me from this. You think that concept in a microsecond. Then you say, 'Yes, sir, Mr. Mulligan. I'll do my best. The problem will be fixed. You can count on it.' Then you think, Whew, Lord! You really do have a problem here. I'm so glad that I don't have to do this rewrite. Yes! The burden is the Lord's! Afterward, you burn the midnight oil, highly motivated as your hands sometimes fly over, sometimes labor over the keyboard of your computer, trusting that Christ is doing this report for you, through you on a moment-by-moment basis. Yes! You don't go fishing and wait till you feel the Spirit of Christ take over and carry you to the computer terminal. You go sit at the keyboard. You save the document to a working file and then begin the rewrite job. However; your faith is saying, 'OK, Lord, where do we begin? I don't have a clue.' This, my friend, is trusting Christ as life through you, by faith. The Christian who fellowships with Christ as I've illustrated in these anecdotes will soon become fast friends with Him."[27]

As we learn to live this way, we will experience the divine dance in heaven and the divine dancers here on earth—us in Christ and Christ in us. So to review, we have to take hold of eternal life, which means we must fall in love with the person, Jesus. We have to believe objective reality in order to experience subjective reality. We have to stop trusting in our own efforts to live the Christian life. And we have to live in abiding prayer, trusting Christ to express His life through us.

Charles Wesley was a prolific hymn writer. He wrote several Christmas carols. Probably his most famous was *Hark the Herald Angels Sing*. I would be willing to bet his least known carol is *Celebrate Immanuel's Name*. I doubt many have ever sung it. I am sure it is never played on Christmas radio stations. But it describes beautifully the idea of the divine dance. Allow me to walk you through the lines of this amazing hymn. I will interrupt the text with a few thoughts here and there.

"Celebrate Immanuel's name, the Prince of

life and peace.
God with us, our lips proclaim, our faithful
hearts confess.
God is in our flesh revealed..."

God revealed in our flesh is another way of saying, Christ in us, the hope of glory.

"Heav'n and earth in Jesus join..."

Jesus is the bridge that joins humanity and divinity together.

"Mortal with Immortal filled, and human
with Divine.
Fullness of the Deity in Jesus' body
dwells..."

Jesus is the visible expression of the invisible God. Through Jesus, God dwelt in His fullness, but Wesley took it a step further and expressed that He brought that partnership into our humanity.

"Dwells in all His saints and me when God
His Son reveals..."

The divine God not only revealed Himself in Jesus, but now He reveals himself in us.

"Father, manifest Thy Son; breathe the true
incarnate Word.
In our inmost souls make known the
presence of the Lord..."

This is a prayer that Jesus would live his life through us.

"Let the Spirit of our Head through every
member flow;

By our Lord inhabited, we then Immanuel
know.
Then He doth His Name express; God in us
we truly prove..."

This is saying God wants to demonstrate His life through us.

"Find with all the life of grace and all the
power of love."[28]

It is a life of grace and love God wants to manifest through us. The title says it all, *Celebrate Immanuel's Name*—that's the joy of the divine dance. We are in Christ and He lives His life through us.

4
It's Not About the Rules

The hope of every disciple is to conquer sin and live a holy life. But what does that mean, and how do we do it? We saw from Scripture that God is love; therefore everything we do must be shaped by that reality. A holy life must flow from that fountain. But growing up, I didn't connect holiness to love. I associated holiness with harsh, unyielding rules and regulations. When I envisioned God I saw a furrowed browed Puritan staring at me with disdain. I grew up in the Pilgrim Holiness Church. That background taught me that holiness was about obedience. Sin was disobedience, and if after committing it, you were unfortunate enough to die before thoroughly repenting, you would be sentenced to an endless torment in the fires of hell. I remember many times the long walk down the isle, trembling as I stepped in rhythm to one more verse of *Just As I Am*. I was on my way to "get saved" for the umpteenth time because I had disobeyed God (I probably thought a cuss word in my mind earlier that week) and needed rescue from the sure destruction that was headed my way if I didn't get right with God. Holiness was about moral purity and obedience. The goal of "growing in grace" (John Wesley's term for discipleship) was to stop sinning and live an obedient life. But I believe that approach to holiness is problematic. It leads to legalism rather than freedom. My spiritual journey was laced with guilt and the fear of eternal doom. I remember having vivid dreams about going to hell, or being possessed by a demon. I associated the way of Christ with fear and judgment rather than joy. But the way of Jesus is the way of life, not legalism. It's the way of joy, not condemnation. My hope is to reframe the discipleship journey so we can see God's true intention for us; walk in the way of joy; experience the abundant life that Jesus promised; and map out a discipleship journey that is grounded in the love of God.

What Is So Sinful About Sin?

I want to start with a definition of sin. The world considers sin an invention of the Church to control people. Blogger, Lisa Kerr, expresses a view that is typical of the culture at large: "The idea of sin is made up by preachers and people who want to perpetuate religion. Is the idea of sin really necessary as a driving force to be a better person? Is guilt necessary to cause us to 'confess' our shortcomings? I don't think so."[29] If we think of sin as simply breaking the rules, then I get Kerr's point of view. However, I believe Scripture demonstrates that something else is going on when we consider the nature of sin. The first place sin is mentioned in the Bible is in its first book, Genesis. It characterizes sin as an enemy waiting to attack. " 'Why are you so angry?' the Lord asked Cain. 'Why do you look so dejected? You will be accepted if you do what is right. But if you refuse to do what is right, then watch out! **Sin is crouching at the door, eager to control you**. But you must subdue it and be its master' "—(Genesis 4:6-7 emphasis added). Moses said sin was waiting to pounce on Cain's heart and drive him to do something terrible. Consequently, he didn't listen to God and was filled with hatred and jealousy that eventually led to the murder of his brother. Sin is a spiritual virus that seeks to destroy our lives. But how do we know when we have sinned? One person may consider a particular action sinful, while another does not.

I have been a pastor in four different states and have noticed that even in the same denomination there are things that are taboo in one area, while perfectly acceptable in another. I spent 22 wonderful years pastoring a church in Maine. From there, we moved to North Carolina. One of the big differences we noticed was how people talked—not just the accents, but even the words are different. Some words we used regularly in Maine are considered vulgar in the South. When speaking of flatulence, for example, we use the word f**t. The first time I said that word in the South, people were shocked because down there, that is a cuss word—a sin. I learned quickly that within the same denomination, sin is viewed differently. In the North, to speak the truth, even if it's blunt, is considered honorable. But in the South, direct honesty is considered rude. It is far better to hide how you really feel if it will be perceived as ungracious, even if that means fudging the truth. To a Northerner that's just plain lying. To a Southerner, that's being gracious. How do we define sin so its definition is universal? John Wesley, the founder of Methodism, defined it as, "a willful transgression against a known law of God."[30] The Dictionary says it is "an immoral act considered to be a transgression against divine law." In other words, the law says don't do that, but we knowingly and willfully choose to do it anyway. God draws a line in the sand and says don't cross. Sin is when we cross the line. But why is it sin? Is it just because God said don't do it? That's like when our parents told us not to do something and we asked why, only to hear them reply, because I said so. I think we have viewed sin in a wrong way. Living in God's will isn't about following orders when our heavenly general issues a command. That is too simplistic and doesn't really get to the heart of what sin is. For example, the Bible says do not lie, but the question is why not? What is it about lying that is sinful? And why is stealing, or breaking the Sabbath, or adultery, or gossip sinful? If we can get to the heart of why it is wrong, then we will better understand what sin is.

What is so sinful about sin? I don't think God issues arbitrary commands and is then ticked off when we disobey them, like the bully who dares us to knock the pack of cigarettes off his shoulder. There is good reason for the things God requires. His desire is that we live in healthy relationship with one another, just as He does within the community of the Trinity. His commands are about relationships, so when we break them, we are doing more than knocking something off His shoulder. We are hurting people. The sinfulness of sin is the violation of relationships—our relationship with God, with self and with others. If we think about the commandments of God, we can see relationship at the heart of them all. For example, the Ten Commandments were a legal code, given to help people live with God and others. The first four deal with our relationship with God, and the last six deal with our relationships with each other.

1. You shall have no other gods before Me.
2. You shall not make idols.
3. You shall not take the name of the LORD your God in vain.
4. Remember the Sabbath day, to keep it holy.
5. Honor your father and your mother.
6. You shall not murder.
7. You shall not commit adultery.

8. You shall not steal.
9. You shall not bear false witness against your neighbor.
10. You shall not covet.[31]

Things like lying, stealing and adultery are wrong, not simply because God said "No," but because they harm relationships. When we break any of those commandments we drive a wedge between us and another person. We will see this same thing in the New Testament. Galatians 5:19-21 lists the deeds of flesh. Every one of them is something that hurts human relationships. "When you follow the desires of your sinful nature, the results are very clear: sexual immorality, impurity, lustful pleasures, idolatry, sorcery, hostility, quarreling, jealousy, outbursts of anger, selfish ambition, dissension, division, envy, drunkenness, wild parties, and other sins like these"— (Galatians 5:19-21). Sexual immorality, impurity and lustful pleasures hurt marriages. Idolatry damages our relationship with God. Sorcery abuses others because it is about manipulating people to gain power. Hostility, quarreling, jealousy, outbursts of anger, selfish ambition, dissension, division, envy all damage human relationships. Drunkenness and wild parties are also listed as destructive—not because God doesn't want us to have fun, but because drunkenness leads to addiction, which destroys marriages and families and leads to personal ruin.

If the churches across America could get hold of this it would change our congregations. Our value systems would be turned up side down. That's because we have often viewed the "big" sins as things like drinking, carousing and smoking, but then we wink at others like gossip, slander and dissension. The institutional church tends to zero in on those sins done openly in bars and nightclubs, while looking the other way at the sins committed in the secret places behind closed doors. However, when we examine the sins God hates, He lists those that affect relationships. "There are six things the Lord hates—no, seven things he detests: haughty eyes, a lying tongue, hands that kill the innocent, a heart that plots evil, feet that race to do wrong, a false witness who pours out lies, a person who sows discord in a family"— (Proverbs 6:16-19). That doesn't say one thing about drunkenness or adultery. That's not to say that adultery or drunkenness is okay. They are wrong too, but they are wrong because they destroy relationships. The sins that are far more damaging are the ones we can easily do in everyday conversation. I have watched churches recover from affairs, divorce and drunk driving charges, but I have also witnessed churches torn apart by gossip, slander and backstabbing. If we understand that sin is violation of relationship then it changes the categories for what we consider the "big" sins and the "tolerable" sins.

The Destructive Power of Sin

Sin causes destruction. The Bible says, "The wages of sin is death"—(Romans 6:23). When we read that verse, we most likely think of hell—that the wages of sin is hell. But often when the Bible speaks of death, though it can mean eternal separation from God, it often is speaking of more immediate destruction. Sin leads to death, but death is separation from God, separation from our selves and separation from others. For example, God told Adam that if he ate from the forbidden tree, he would die. God said, "But from the tree of the knowledge of good and evil you shall not eat, for **in the day** that you eat from it you will surely die"—(Genesis 2:17 emphasis added). The problem is, Adam didn't die. In fact, he lived many years after that. "Adam lived 930 years, and then he died"—(Genesis 5:5). Did God lie? No. Death began in Adam the moment he sinned. What God said was that the process of death would begin in him. Young's Literal Translation of the Bible fleshes this out better than most. "And of the tree of knowledge of good and evil, thou dost not eat of it, for in the day of thine eating of it—dying thou dost die"—(Genesis 2:17 YLT). Notice that last phrase. It said, "dying thou dost die". It means, in dying you will die. The process of death began in Adam the day he sinned. When a branch is cut from a tree, the leaves on the branch are still green. In time they will turn brittle and brown because they are separated from their source of life. That is what happened to Adam. He was severed from the source of life and the process of death began in him. Death is ultimately separation of the spirit from the body (James 2:26), but that downward spiral began immediately. First, Adam hid from God. Notice, by the way, that God did not hide from Adam. In fact, God sought him out (Genesis 3:9). But in Adam's heart there was a distance between him and God, so he hid himself. There was also a separation between him and Eve. Immediately when God began to question them, Adam threw her under the bus. He blamed her for his choice to sin. Almost immediately he was hiding and blaming.

Sin creates its own destruction. "Those who live only to satisfy their own sinful nature will harvest decay and death from that sinful nature"—(Galatians 6:8). Sin will divide friendships and families. It destroys everything beautiful about humanity. When God takes His hands off and leaves people to themselves, sin totally disrupts society. Notice how Paul describes it. "Since they thought it foolish to acknowledge God, he abandoned them to their foolish thinking and let them do things that should never be done. Their lives became full of every kind of wickedness, sin, greed, hate, envy, murder, quarreling, deception, malicious behavior, and gossip. They are backstabbers, haters of God, insolent, proud, and boastful. They invent new ways of sinning, and they disobey their parents. They refuse to understand, break their promises, are heartless, and have no mercy. They know God's justice requires that those who do these things deserve to die, yet they do them anyway. Worse yet, they encourage others to do them, too"—(Romans 1:28-32).

The True Focus of Holiness

If sin is violation of relationship, then holiness is living in right relationship with God and others. I had always thought of holiness as not breaking the rules. But it cannot be that, because God is holy. God has always been holy, and yet, there was a time before men and angels were created when there was no sin, no law, no commandments, no rules, and yet God was still holy. Holiness is not observed by contrasting it with sin. Holiness is found within the relationship of the Trinity. When we look there, we see perfect love shared between the Three Persons of the Godhead. Because holiness is more about relationship than rules explains why there were times when Jesus pushed the boundaries of the religious laws of His day. He encouraged

His disciples to eat grain on the Sabbath, which although not a direct violation of the Law, was considered taboo in Jewish society. When challenged about it by the Pharisees, Jesus referenced King David and how he and his men ate the shewbread in the meeting place in the priestly city of Nob. David and his men stopped in Nob while fleeing from Saul. They were hungry, but the priests told him they had no food. All they could offer was the bread in the sanctuary, which was restricted from any use other than worship. In raising this issue as a defense for His disciples, Jesus was endorsing what David did. David clearly broke the Law, but it was justified to satisfy a human need, and Jesus was in total support of that action. When a woman was caught in adultery and thrown at Jesus' feet, the Pharisees demanded He decide her fate. The Law required she be stoned, but they wanted to know what Jesus thought. He had preached a message of love and mercy, so if He sided with the Law, they could accuse Him of hypocrisy. If He let her go, they could accuse Him of lawlessness. Jesus responded by instructing the one among them without sin to cast the first stone. No one would ever admit that, so one by one they left until there was only Jesus and the woman. He told her directly He was not going to condemn her. He let her go. He encouraged her not to sin anymore, but He did not keep the letter of the Law and demand her death, because the spirit of the Law was more important than the letter.

Jesus drew a lot of criticism because He hung out with drunks and prostitutes. He spent time with them and I am sure people whispered about what they thought was really happening. Let's be honest, if we hung around with prostitutes, do you think the people who see us would think we were just doing crossword puzzles? Jesus was accused of partying and engaging in extra-curricular activities. But Jesus hung out with them because they were spiritually sick and He had the cure. He said a physician doesn't hang out with people who are well, but instead with those who need a doctor. But His critics couldn't get their heads around that. An acquaintance of mine shared with me once that while in Boston, he hired a prostitute. When she got in his car he paid her for an hour and asked if they could do whatever he wanted within reason. She said she was his for an hour. She was ready to drive off to find a hotel, but he pulled over and stopped the car. He told her he just wanted to talk, and then for the next hour he shared the gospel with her. She was on the clock and getting paid, so she stayed there and listened. When he told me this, he swore me to secrecy because the community he lived in would have never understood what he was doing. He feared rejection and condemnation, because "good church people" don't hang out with prostitutes. But Jesus did. And so did my friend. It may not "appear" acceptable to religious folk, but relationship always trumps law.

Look, for example, at Rahab the prostitute who hid Joshua's spies when they were checking out Jericho. She was honored for helping Joshua's spies. She was even included in the genealogy of Jesus. It was unprecedented for a woman to appear in a Jewish genealogy, let alone a pagan prostitute. But the first book of the New Testament places her in the heart of the action. "Salmon was the father of Boaz (whose mother was Rahab). Boaz was the father of Obed (whose mother was Ruth). Obed was the father of Jesse"—(Matthew 1:5). Rahab is found in the great faith chapter of Hebrews. "It was by faith that Rahab the prostitute was not destroyed with the people in her city who refused to obey God. For she had given a friendly welcome to the spies"—(Hebrews 11:31). And James, the Lord's brother, lifted her up as an example. "Rahab the prostitute is another example. She was shown to be right with God by her actions when she hid those messengers and sent them safely away by a different road"—(James 2:25). Notice James says her actions demonstrated her righteousness. What were her actions? She hid the spies. But how did she do that? She lied. She told a bald-faced lie to the King's guards. "Then Joshua secretly sent out two spies from the Israelite camp at Acacia Grove. He instructed them, 'Scout out the land on the other side of the Jordan River, especially around Jericho.' So the two men set out and came to the house of a prostitute named Rahab and stayed there that night. But someone told the king of Jericho, 'Some Israelites have come here tonight to spy out the land.' So the king of Jericho sent orders to Rahab: 'Bring out the men who have come into your house, for they have come here to spy out the whole land.' Rahab had hidden the two men, but she replied, 'Yes, the men were here earlier, but I didn't know where they were from. [that's a lie] They left the town at dusk [that's a lie], as the gates were about to close. I don't know where they went [another lie]. If you hurry, you can probably catch up with them [and another lie]"—(Joshua 2:1-5). She lied, but she was honored because relationship trumps rules. God forbids lying, but hospitality and relationship with Joshua's spies took precedence—relationship over rules. Jesus made this clear in His grand-sweeping statement to a Law expert who questioned Him. "'Teacher, which is the most important commandment in the Law of Moses?' Jesus replied, " 'You must love the Lord your God with all your heart, all your soul, and all your mind.' This is the first and greatest commandment. A second is equally important: 'Love your neighbor as yourself.' **The entire law and all the demands of the prophets are based on these two commandments**"—(Matthew 22:36-40 emphasis added).

Radical Implications for a Discipleship Plan

Sin is the violation of relationship. Holiness is living in right relationship with God and man. The discipleship journey is about learning to live a holy life, and that therefore means learning how to live in right relationship with God and others. The goal of discipleship is not Bible reading, prayer, tithing, ministry or church attendance. It's not that they are unimportant, but they are a means to an end. Some people think if they read their Bible and pray everyday, they are moving forward in the discipleship journey, but that is not necessarily true. The Bible and prayer are tools to help us grow in our relationship with Jesus, so that He can share His life through us, so that our relationships will be whole and healthy. The goal of discipleship is about living in harmony with God, spouse, children, family, co-workers, neighbors, friends and strangers—It's about relationships. Are they healthy and whole? That's how we measure spiritual maturity.

When the Bible lists the requirements for spiritual leaders, it leans heavily on relationships. "I left you on the island of Crete so you could complete our work there and appoint elders in each town as I instructed you. An elder must live a blameless life. He must be faithful to his wife, and his children must be believers who don't have a reputation for being wild or rebellious. An elder is a manager of God's household, so he must live a blameless life. He must not be arrogant or quick-tempered; he must not be a heavy drinker, violent, or dishonest with money. Rather, he must enjoy having guests in his home, and he must love what is good. He must live wisely and be just. He must live a devout and disciplined life. He must have a strong belief in the trustworthy message he was taught; then he will be able to encourage others with wholesome teaching and show those who oppose it where they are wrong"—(Titus 1:5-9). Even though that list includes teaching and living a pure life, it is centered on relationships—with spouse, children, church and community.

How Holiness Is Displayed

Holiness is about relationships, and the measure of healthy relationships is the fruit of the Spirit manifested in those relationships. Holiness is displayed by love, joy, peace, patience, kindness, goodness, faithfulness, gentleness and self-control. When we say Jesus wants to live through us, we mean He wants to manifest His joy, peace, patience, and all the other characteristics of His nature through our lives. He wants those qualities of His Spirit to shape and flavor our relationships. The key to the Christian life is allowing Jesus to manifest those fruit through our lives into our relationships, but there are barriers we put up that block the flow of the Spirit. With each fruit there are deeds of the flesh that hinder the flow of the Spirit. Paul mentioned them in Galatians. "Sexual immorality, impurity, lustful pleasures, idolatry, sorcery, hostility, quarreling, jealousy, outbursts of anger, selfish ambition, dissension, division, envy, drunkenness, wild parties, and other sins like these. Let me tell you again, as I have before, that anyone living that sort of life will not inherit the Kingdom of God"— (Galatians 5:19-21).

Each of those deeds stand opposed to the manifestation of God's character. Love is blocked by impurity and lustful pleasures. Joy, which speaks of inner contentment, is stymied by idolatry, sorcery and envy. Hostility stands opposed to peace. Patience is tested by quarreling. Selfish ambition and dissension fight against kindness. Jealousy and division work to stamp out goodness. Gentleness, which is power under control, is opposed by outbursts of anger. Sexual immorality attacks faithfulness, and self-control is eroded by drunkenness and wild parties. The Holy Spirit can be grieved and actually hindered from flowing through our lives when we give into these fleshly activities. Notice how Paul connected the dots between the grieving of the Holy Spirit and hurtful relationships. "And do not bring sorrow to God's Holy Spirit by the way you live. Remember, he has identified you as his own, guaranteeing that you will be saved on the day of redemption. Get rid of all bitterness, rage, anger, harsh words, and slander, as well as all types of evil behavior. Instead, be kind to each other, tenderhearted, forgiving one another, just as God through Christ has forgiven you"—(Ephesians 4:30-32).

The Journey Ahead

The discipleship process is to discover the barriers in our lives for each area of fruit and remove them so Jesus can flow through us in that area. In the chapters that follow, we will look at the manifestation of a particular fruit in Jesus' life and how it was seen in His relationships. For example, when looking at the fruit of patience, we will look at how Jesus displayed patience with those around Him, and from that, we will develop a practical definition of that fruit. We will then look at the various barriers that can stop the flow of that fruit. For example we will ask, what stops Jesus' patience from flowing through our lives? We will ask questions about our relationships that will help us identify which barriers are hindering healthy relationships in our lives—which barriers keep the fruit of Jesus' Spirit from flowing into our relationships. Those barriers will then become our tailor fit discipleship plan. We will learn how to claim Christ's crucifixion over those areas of our lives, and trust Jesus to flow through us in that area. The hope is that such a journey will bring healing and health to our various relationships.

Fruit or Flesh

There is one more thing we have to do, however, before we start examining each individual fruit. There is one fruit in the list of nine that is predominant and affects all the others—love. We have to first understand love's place in the list of fruit so we can also understand the one enemy that will try to shut it down. We saw that death is about separation from ourselves, from others and ultimately, from God. God's mission was to bring unity where death separates. "And all of this is a gift from God, **who brought us back to himself** through Christ. And God has given us this task of **reconciling** people to him. For God was in Christ, **reconciling** the world to himself, no longer counting people's sins against them. And he gave us this wonderful message of **reconciliation**"—(2 Corinthians 5:18-19 emphasis added). Reconciliation means to join, to unite. God takes what is dead (separated) and brings it back together. The way Jesus reconciled us was through love. His love had the power to undo death—as the Song of Solomon says, "Love is as strong as death"— (Song 8:6). Jesus destroyed death with love. He removed separation with love. He united division with love.

Mixed Messages About Love

Jesus, however, faced a great challenge. He lived in a society that had mixed messages about love. The Jews were intensely committed to family, but pushed others away. Women were considered second-class citizens, not even being allowed to testify in a court of law, as their witness was not considered credible. Slavery was practiced and slaves were viewed as little more than property. Racism was encouraged. Gentiles (non-Jews) and especially Samaritans were despised. A proper Jew would never marry outside their kind, and Gentiles would not be welcome in their home. It was considered an offense to have a Gentile under one's roof.

God wanted Peter to minister to a Gentile named Cornelius, but He took the time to prepare Peter for his assignment. Peter had a dream about a sheet with many kinds of animals in it. The sheet was lowered from heaven and God told him to eat. Peter refused because some of the animals were ceremonially unclean. Peter, being a good Jew, had never allowed any unclean animal to touch his lips. But God insisted, telling Peter that what God calls clean is clean. And now, by His decree all animals were considered clean. When Peter awoke, the Holy Spirit told him that a Gentile was sending a message to him to seek his help. He would ask Peter to come to his home, and Peter was to agree. It was an elaborate method necessary to help Peter overcome his prejudice. While at Cornelius' home, the Holy Spirit fell on the group and they began to speak in tongues, just as the Jews had on the Day of Pentecost. That signified to Peter that God was opening salvation to the Gentiles. The church in Jerusalem was reluctant to accept that Gentiles could be part of God's church. It was only the Pentecostal miracle of tongues that convinced them the way of Christ was not exclusive to the Jews.

There was an unofficial caste system in Jesus' day. People who were sick were considered under the judgment of God. It was believed that they, or someone related to them, must have done something sinful to deserve their disease. Their biased feelings come through in a conversation the disciples had with Jesus over a blind man. "As Jesus was walking along, he saw a man who had been blind from birth. 'Rabbi,' his disciples asked him, 'why was this man born blind? Was it because of his own sins or his parents' sins?'"—(John 9:1-2).

The Foundational Fruit

Jesus came into a bigoted, prejudicial, divided world to live the perfect life of love on our behalf. And through His Holy Spirit He now wants to live that life through us. That's what the fruit of the Spirit is all about. It describes how Jesus wants to express His nature through our lives. "But the Holy Spirit produces this kind of fruit in our lives: love, joy, peace, patience, kindness, goodness, faithfulness, gentleness, and self-control"—(Galatians 5:22-23). There are nine different fruit listed in this passage. They are describing the different facets of Jesus' nature. He wants to express His life through us and this is what that looks like. But even though there are nine qualities listed, love is the predominate quality, and all the others are different manifestations of love. You can see this by comparing the fruit of the Spirit with 1 Corinthians 13:4-7: "Love is patient and kind. Love is not jealous or boastful or proud or rude. It does not demand its own way. It is not irritable, and it keeps no record of being wronged. It does not rejoice about injustice but rejoices whenever the truth wins out. Love never gives up, never loses faith, is always hopeful, and endures through every circumstance." In the chart below I have matched up each fruit with the corresponding line in the Corinthian description of love.

Galatians 5:22-23	1 Corinthians 13:4-7
Love	Love is…
Joy	Rejoices whenever truth wins out
Peace	It is not irritable, and it keeps no record of being wronged
Patience	Love is patient
Kindness	Love is kind
goodness	Is not jealous or boastful or rude
Gentleness	It does not demand its own way
Faithfulness	Never gives up; never loses faith
Self-control	endures through every circumstance

The reason they match up so well is because love is the foundational fruit. Love holds all the other fruit together. The ESV translation of Colossians 3:12-13 states this clearly: "Put on then, as God's chosen ones, holy and beloved, compassionate hearts, kindness, humility, meekness, and patience, bearing with one another and, if one has a complaint against another, forgiving each other; as the Lord has forgiven you, so you also must forgive. And above all these put on love, **which binds everything together in perfect harmony**"—(ESV emphasis added). Philip D. Kenneson in his book, *Life on the Vine* explains that love is like a prism that takes the light in and divides it into the colors of the rainbow.[32] He quotes Stephen F. Winward who writes, "In this sense, love is much like light which, when passing through a prism, breaks into its component colors."[33] We are really studying different aspects of love when we study the different fruit. It makes sense that love would be the foundational fruit, because it is the very heart of God. As we saw earlier, the Apostle John wrote, "God is love"—(1 John 4:8). This is why the whole heart of Christianity is summarized in love. "So now faith, hope, and love abide, these three; but the greatest of these is love"—(1 Corinthians 13:13).

Jesus' Life a Total Expression of Love

Jesus' life was a total expression of love. His teaching was radical because it taught a love that was unheard of in His culture. In the famous Sermon on the Mount, Jesus taught His listeners to love beyond their circle, to love even their enemies. "You have heard that it was said, 'You shall love your neighbor and hate your enemy.' But I say to you, love your enemies and pray for those who persecute you, so that you may be sons of your Father who is in heaven. For he makes his sun rise on the evil and on the good, and sends rain on the just and on the unjust. For if you love those who love you, what reward do you have? Do not even the tax collectors do the same? And if you greet only your brothers, what more are you doing than others? Do not even the Gentiles do the same?"—(Matthew 5:43-47).

Jesus taught in stories and though we enjoy His keen perception of life, His stories were scandalous. When we track along with one of Jesus' most popular parables, (Luke 10:25-37) and read it as His original audience would have heard it, we can see just how counter-cultural and offensive it would have been. "And behold, a lawyer stood up to put him to the test"—(10:25a). This was not the type of lawyer we have in our society, but rather this was referring to an expert in the Biblical Law. The text goes on to say: "'Teacher, what shall I do to inherit eternal life?' He said to him, 'What is written in the Law? How do you read it?' And he answered, 'You shall love the Lord your God with all your heart and with all your soul and with all your strength and with all your mind, and your neighbor as yourself.' And he said to him, 'You have answered correctly; do this, and you will live'"—(10:25b-28). The Lawyer answered perfectly because he knew the summation of the Law was to love. But he pressed Jesus further. "But he, desiring to justify himself, said to Jesus, 'And who is my neighbor?'"—(10:29). He was trying to back Jesus into a corner, and in response, this is where Jesus told His story.

An Offensive Parable

"A man was going down from Jerusalem to Jericho, and he fell among robbers, who stripped him and beat him and departed, leaving him half dead. Now by chance a priest was going down that road, and when he saw him he passed by on the other side"—(10:30-31). A priest was a highly regarded member of Jewish society. He was considered a holy man, but he totally ignored the stranger in need. Right away Jesus was stepping on shaky ground because He painted the priest in an unfavorable light. But Jesus poked the beehive even more. "So likewise a Levite, when he came to the place and saw him, passed by on the other side"—(10:32). A Levite was a member of the priestly line. All priests had to be from the family of Levi. This man who was an expert in the Law was probably a Levite. He did the same thing as the priest; ignored the man in need. Then Jesus said something completely offensive. "But a Samaritan, as he journeyed, came to where he was, and when he saw him, he had compassion. He went to him and bound up his wounds, pouring on oil and wine. Then he set him on his own animal and brought him to an inn and took care of him. And the next day he took out two denarii and gave them to the innkeeper, saying, 'Take care of him, and whatever more you spend, I will repay you when I come back'"—(10:33-35). Jesus committed an unforgiveable social taboo. He made the despised Samaritan a better person than the two Jews. But still, He was not done. The next thing He did pulled the rug out from under the lawyer. When we read the story up to this point, we assume the neighbor is the guy who got mugged and we are supposed to love him, but Jesus asked the lawyer a question that turned the situation completely on its head. "'Which of these three, do you think, proved to be a neighbor to the man who fell among the robbers?' He said, 'The one who showed him mercy'"—(10:36-37). Jesus took the guy who was mugged off the table. The neighbor had to be one of the three who encountered the mugged man. The obvious answer was the despised Samaritan. But notice the lawyer couldn't bring himself to say the word Samaritan. He could only force out, "the one who showed him mercy." I love it! So when the Lawyer asked Jesus who his neighbor was, who he should love, Jesus' answer was the Samaritan. Jesus implied that the lawyer was to love the one who functioned like a neighbor, and that was the Samaritan. In other words, love your enemies, not just those in your circle of family and friends. He wrapped up His encounter with the admonition, "You go, and do likewise"—(10:37). Jesus taught us to love those outside our circle.

Jesus Practiced Counter-cultural Love

But Jesus didn't just teach about it. He practiced it. He hung out with tax collectors, prostitutes and sinners. Mark tells us in his gospel account, "And as he reclined at table in his house, many tax collectors and sinners were reclining with Jesus and his disciples, for there were many who followed him"—(Mark 2:15). He crossed racial lines by healing people outside the Jewish community. A Syrophoenician woman brought her daughter to Jesus because she was demon possessed. When she asked Jesus to heal her, Jesus replied as a typical Jew would have in that day. First He ignored her. But when she persisted, He commented that it would not be proper to give the master's food to dogs. He called her a Gentile dog! But instead of being offended, she countered by saying that even the dogs get to eat the crumbs at the master's table. He was moved by her faith and healed her daughter. He used His words to underscore the stereotype of the typical Jew, but healed the girl to demonstrate His love was atypical.

Jesus loved those who were shunned by society. Lepers were sequestered from everyone for fear of spreading their horrible disease. When walking in a crowd they were to cry, "Unclean! Unclean!" so people would steer clear. Their own words forced them to participate in their own shunning. But when Jesus encountered them, He did not steer clear. Matthew tells a moving story about Jesus' encounter with a leper. "When he came down from the mountain, great crowds followed him. And behold, a leper came to him and knelt before him, saying, 'Lord, if you will, you can make me clean.' And Jesus stretched out his hand and touched him, saying, 'I will; be clean.' And immediately his leprosy was cleansed"—(Matthew 3:1-3). It is easy to read past this story and miss something incredibly important. Jesus didn't just heal the man; He touched him. He reached out and made physical contact. It may have been the first time in years anyone dared to grace the man with a human touch. He didn't just need physical healing, he needed emotional healing and Jesus gave it. He loved those who were rejected by others.

He confronted the misogynistic culture of His day by treating women with dignity. Women were considered second-class citizens. They were not even allowed to testify in a court of law because their word was considered unreliable. Men would not have spent time talking with women in public. But one day while outside the borders of Israel Jesus sat by a well, while His disciples went into town to get some food. While there, a Samaritan woman approached. She was there to draw water in the middle of the day. The women had the task of carrying water from the well to their homes. Usually they would carry the water in the cool of the day, either in the morning or the evening, but not during the middle of the day. The fact that this woman was coming in the afternoon indicates she was not welcome to travel along with the other women. She was shunned. We learn from the gospel account the reason was probably because she lived an immoral lifestyle and was most likely not accepted by the other women. This woman had three strikes against her in terms of ever having a conversation with Jesus. She was female. She was a Gentile, and she was a woman of ill repute. And yet, Jesus took time to speak with her. He introduced her to eternal life. She was so overjoyed by the kindness and help He gave her, she left her water pot to run home and tell her friends about Jesus. Water pots were not items easily discarded. Water was especially precious in that desert climate. People didn't have an abundance of pots lying around their homes. For her to leave her pot there, where someone might take it, was extraordinary.

Water Pots and Harpoons

My favorite TV program is Yukon Men. The program follows the people living in a small town in Tanana, Alaska. They live a subsistence lifestyle. They trap, hunt and fish for their food. When I watch it, I think if I were young, strong, and knowledgeable about the wild and had the money, I would totally move to Alaska and attempt to live off the grid. But I am old, ignorant and could never do it at this stage of life. So I live vicariously through the men and women who tackle the harsh conditions. (It's pathetic, I know. But I can't help myself. I love the show.) Charlie, one of the characters, was ice fishing with his son, Bob, on the Tanana River. He had taught his son to always strap the harpoon to his wrist so that when he thrust it through the hole in the ice, he wouldn't lose it. Of course, his son forgot and the harpoon was lost under the ice in the frigid waters. Charlie couldn't just walk to the local hardware store and buy a new one. There are no hardware stores in Tanana. There are no roads connecting Tanana to another town. (Since the airing of this episode there has actually been a road built to connect Tanana to Fairbanks). The harpoon is essential for catching fish and thus, eating. So Charlie had to teach his son a wilderness survival lesson he wouldn't forget. They opened the hole wide enough for a human to fit through. Bob stripped down to his shorts. Charlie held on to his legs and lowered Bob into the icy river to fish out the harpoon. The first time down, Bob missed. It took two or three tries before Bob got the harpoon. Actually, it was kind of awful to watch, but Bob learned the lesson. They quickly wrapped blankets around Bob and got him before a fire to keep hypothermia from setting in. When you lose a harpoon in Alaska, you go after it. You don't leave them lying around. When in the desert of Samaria, you don't leave a water pot lying around. The fact that she did shows the Samaritan woman was overwhelmed by the love Jesus showed her.

A Scandalous Birth

Jesus willingly stepped into a situation that brought him constant scorn. He arranged the particulars of His birth knowing He would be the brunt of gossip for His entire life. Mary was pregnant out of wedlock. It was a miracle of the Holy Spirit, but nobody believed that. Even Joseph, her betrothed, planned to divorce her when he found out she was pregnant. His first and natural assumption was she had slept with another man. Who wouldn't think that? Until a visit from an angel set him straight, he had planned to send her away. If Joseph didn't believe Mary, you can bet no one else did either—and they didn't have angels visiting them to reassure them of the truth. Mary, Joseph and Jesus were the center of town gossip; either, Joseph and Mary slept together before they were married, or Mary got in trouble with someone else. Regardless of how it happened, Jesus was illegitimate in their eyes. At social gatherings people whispered behind their backs. And the rumors stayed with Jesus His entire life. He was a reject right from the start. The New Testament reveals hints of the scorn Jesus endured.

Son of the Father

Throughout Scripture people were identified by their fathers' name. For example, Matthew 4:21 says, "And going on from there he saw two other brothers, James the son of Zebedee and John his brother, in the boat with Zebedee their father, mending their nets, and he called them". James and John are identified as the sons of Zebedee. The phrase, "son of", occurs over one thousand times in the Bible. In every case the person is identified as the son of their father; in every case that is, except for Jesus. Shortly after launching His ministry the townsfolk were talking about Him. "Jesus left that part of the country and returned with his disciples to Nazareth, his hometown. The next Sabbath he began teaching in the synagogue, and many who heard him were amazed. They asked, 'Where did he get all this wisdom and the power to perform such miracles?' Then they scoffed, 'He's just a carpenter, the son of Mary and the brother of James, Joseph, Judas, and Simon. And his sisters live right here among us.' They were deeply offended and refused to believe in him"—(Mark 6:1-3). The people were offended. He grew up among them and had always been a reject, an illegitimate child. So who does He think He is launching a public ministry? When they said, "He's just a carpenter" they were acknowledging He had learned a skilled trade. That trade was learned from His stepfather, Joseph. But they never mention Him. Instead, they referred to Him as the son of Mary. After 30 years, and in spite of His great wisdom, He still carried the scorn of illegitimacy.

That reputation went beyond Nazareth. The religious leaders in Jerusalem hurled the same insults at Him. Jesus was debating them when the issue of parentage came up. Jesus said, " 'Yes, I realize that you are descendants of Abraham. And yet some of you are trying to kill me because there's no room in your hearts for my message. I am telling you what I saw when I was with my Father. But you are following the advice of your father.' 'Our father is Abraham!' they declared. 'No,' Jesus replied, 'for if you were really the children of Abraham, you would follow his example. Instead, you are trying to kill me because I told you the truth, which I heard from God. Abraham never did such a thing. No, you are imitating your real father.' They replied, 'We aren't illegitimate children! God himself is our true Father' "—(John 8:38-41). The implication is clear; Jesus is illegitimate. Jesus willingly submitted Himself to scorn and ridicule. He planned His own birth and knew how others would react to it. He was willing to do that because love is always other centered. His mission, purpose and focus was to rescue us from sin, and subjecting Himself to ridicule and scorn was part of the necessary path He had to take to secure our salvation.

Love Versus Lust

The Apostle Paul wrote, "Don't be selfish; don't try to impress others. Be humble, thinking of others as better than yourselves. Don't look out only for your own interests, but take an interest in others, too.

You must have the same attitude that Christ Jesus had. Though he was God, he did not think of equality with God as something to cling to. Instead, he gave up his divine privileges; he took the humble position of a slave and was born as a human being. When he appeared in human form, he humbled himself in obedience to God and died a criminal's death on a cross"—(Philippians 2:3-8). Notice, Paul began this section by saying, "Don't be selfish". Selfishness is the enemy of love. In fact, the opposite of love is not hate, as is commonly thought. The opposite of love is lust. Lust is more than sexual desire. Lust is an inward focus, the ultimate expression of selfishness. A lust focus makes everything about me; life is about what I want, when I want it, the way I want it. Love, on the other hand, is outward focused. It puts the needs of others first. Paul showed in this paragraph that Jesus lived with a love focus, and was warning us against its opposite—selfishness.

Paul identified this lust focus as the flesh, or in other places as the sinful nature. When we become followers of Christ a battle ensues between our flesh and God's Spirit. The flesh tries to stop the fruit of God's Spirit from flowing through our lives. "So I say, let the Holy Spirit guide your lives. Then you won't be doing what your sinful nature craves"—(Galatians 5:16). Paul said we have a nature that has cravings. The word translated as "craves" means "to desire, to long, to want what is forbidden, to lust". He went on to say, "The sinful nature [Paul's word for the lust focus] wants to do evil, which is just the opposite of what the Spirit wants. And the Spirit gives us desires that are the opposite of what the sinful nature desires. These two forces are constantly fighting each other"—(5:16-17). There is a constant battle within us and we need to know how to win it, so that the love of Jesus can flow through our lives. Paul finished the paragraph by saying, "You are not free to carry out your good intentions"—(5:17). We have good intentions to be loving people, but our sinful, self-focused nature stands in the way. So we have to learn how to battle it. This is all tied to our study of the fruit of the Spirit, because, in the very next paragraph Paul described both the fruit of the Spirit and the deeds of the flesh. "When you follow the desires of your sinful nature, the results are very clear: sexual immorality, impurity, lustful pleasures, idolatry, sorcery, hostility, quarreling, jealousy, outbursts of anger, selfish ambition, dissension, division, envy, drunkenness, wild parties, and other sins like these. Let me tell you again, as I have before, that anyone living that sort of life will not inherit the Kingdom of God. But the Holy Spirit produces this kind of fruit in our lives: love, joy, peace, patience, kindness, goodness, faithfulness, gentleness, and self-control. There is no law against these things! Those who belong to Christ Jesus have nailed the passions and desires of their sinful nature to his cross and crucified them there. Since we are living by the Spirit, let us follow the Spirit's leading in every part of our lives"—(5:19-25).

Love is the foundational fruit and all the others are expressions of love. In the same way, lust (the flesh) is the foundational deed of the flesh and all the other deeds are expressions of that. So if we are going to fight the individual deeds of the flesh we are going to have to deal with the flesh in general. So as we begin to look at the barriers that keep the fruit from flowing through our lives, the first thing we have to deal with is the flesh. We start by learning to recognize our own selfishness. It's not "if" we are selfish, because we all are to one degree or another. The issue is rather, how often we live with a self-focused orientation. On a scale of 1-10 with 1 being completely self-absorbed and 10 being totally other's focused, like Mother Theresa—where do you think you fall? I suspect many would place themselves somewhere between a 5 or 7. But if asked the same question about their spouse or partner, many would place that person at a 4 or 6. The number would be higher or lower depending on how troubled the relationship was. But in almost every case, we believe our own number would be higher than our spouse's. That's because we are often blinded to our own selfish tendencies.

A Lust Quiz

I want to give you a quiz to help you recognize your own level of selfishness. This quiz will not be a list of questions, because our own hearts will answer them in a way that benefits us. I know this because over many years of pastoral counseling, it has been amazing to hear two people describe the same conflict. Each has an incredible ability to interpret the situation, and share a perspective that makes them look like the victim and the other the villain. It almost never fails. I always have to remember Solomon's advice. "The first to speak in court sounds right—until the cross-examination begins"—(Proverbs 18:17). I'll hear his story and think, that poor guy. But then I'll hear her account and think, how can she live with him? People are skilled at painting themselves in the most favorable light. It's not because they are dishonest, but rather because we tend to be blind to our own issues. Instead, I propose a more honest quiz. I want to challenge you to do some things over the next month that will open your eyes to you.

1. One of the characteristics of a selfish person is they always put self first.[34] Try doing the following over the next month: The next time you're doing something, whether you're in line at a buffet or racing to get that open spot in the line at the grocery store, let the other person go in front of you. If you're in traffic and others are trying to merge in, be the one who lets them in the lane. Make a goal of putting yourself last in at least three situations this week. Pay attention to how many times you do it, or how many times you pass because you are in a hurry and your schedule is more important than theirs.

2. Selfish people ignore everyone else's perspective and think only of their own. You've heard the cliché about walking a mile in another person's moccasins; put the effort into thinking about the other people around you and considering how they might be feeling in any given situation. For example, if you ordered a baked potato at your local restaurant, and the waitress brings mashed, think about what she may be going through before complaining. She could be exhausted from rushing on her feet for many hours, or perhaps she received bad news from that doctor that day and her mind is understandably somewhere else. Try being kind, because you have no idea what she is going through. She certainly doesn't need a grouchy customer making her day any worse.

3. Selfish people are always focused on what they want. Over the next month when going out or hanging with others, let them

choose the restaurant, or the movie. Make the decision now to defer to others, and be happy about their choices.

4. Selfish people are reluctant to sacrifice time, effort or money to help others. Take the time to listen to your friends and to observe them. See if you can perceive a need without them asking you for help, and then actually help them. Or ask yourself how willing you are to volunteer somewhere and then see if in the next month you actually do it.

After a month you will get a decent idea of your level of selfishness vs. selflessness. Once we get a sense of the problem with the flesh and are prepared to accept that, we can then present ourselves to the Lord as in Romans 12:1-2. "And so, dear brothers and sisters, I plead with you to give your bodies to God because of all he has done for you. Let them be a living and holy sacrifice—the kind he will find acceptable. This is truly the way to worship him. Don't copy the behavior and customs of this world, but let God transform you into a new person by changing the way you think. Then you will learn to know God's will for you, which is good and pleasing and perfect." This is a reckoning of ourselves as dead, via the death and resurrection of Jesus. It is already done in Christ, but we are getting in line with the truth. According to the word, we are dead and our lives are hidden with Christ in God. We have to come to the place where we settle the issue of self. Paul expressed this idea when he wrote, "It is no longer I who live, but Christ lives in me"—(Galatians 2:20). Having settled that, we are ready to look at each fruit and face the different expressions of self that stop that fruit from flowing in our lives. We will have to remind ourselves that we have died to the flesh each time we face one of the barriers that stand against a particular fruit. Remember, each fruit has corresponding deeds of the flesh that stand opposed to their full expression in our lives. Joy, which is contentment, is opposed by idolatry, sorcery, envy. Peace is opposed by hostility. Patience is hindered by quarreling. Kindness is hindered by selfish ambition and dissension. Goodness is opposed by jealousy and division. Gentleness, which is power under control, is squelched by outbursts of anger.

Sexual immorality stands opposed to faithfulness. And drunkenness and wild parties work against self-control. Each one of those deeds of the flesh are powered by selfishness. So each time we confront one of them, we have to remind ourselves of our death in Christ: "you have died and your life is hidden with Christ in God"—(Colossians 3:3). We have to make sure we are committed to that every time. Are we dead to the flesh? Yes. In Christ, it is a finished reality. We share in His death, because of our union with Him. The more challenging question is, are we willing to act like it? That's what living a crucified life is all about. "Then he said to the crowd, 'If any of you wants to be my follower, you must turn from your selfish ways, take up your cross daily, and follow me. If you try to hang on to your life, you will lose it. But if you give up your life for my sake, you will save it' "—(Luke 9:23-24).

That can be scary. That's why we must know how much God loves us. We can trust Him to look out for our best interests when we choose to lay our interests aside for the sake of others. Understanding God's love for us will lead to experiencing His power within us. "Then Christ will make his home in your hearts as you trust in him. Your roots will grow down into God's love and keep you strong. And may you have **the power to understand**, as all God's people should, **how wide, how long, how high, and how deep his love is**. May you experience the love of Christ, though it is too great to understand fully. **Then** you will be made complete with all the fullness of life **and power** that comes from God"—(Ephesians 3:17-19 emphasis added).

5
Jesus' Joy

"But the Holy Spirit produces this kind of fruit in our lives: love, joy, peace, patience, kindness, goodness, faithfulness, gentleness, and self-control. There is no law against these things"—(Galatians 5:22-23).

Love is the foundational fruit and all the others are different facets of love. Of the remaining eight listed, joy is the first. The fruit of the Spirit represents the different ways Jesus wants to express His love through us. He wants His joy to flow through our lives and affect our relationships. Our marriages, families and friendships will be healthier if Jesus' joy is flowing through us. But when people think of Jesus they often don't think of joy. A cursory glance of the Bible could lead one to conclude Jesus was very serious, burdened and even sad. Isaiah prophesied the Messiah would be "a man of sorrows, acquainted with deepest grief"—(Isaiah 53:3). On one occasion Jesus said His soul was burdened to the point of death, and He was so distressed He sweat drops of blood (Matthew 26:38; Luke 22:44). On another occasion the Bible says Jesus wept (John 11:35). Jesus knelt in front of a large crowd and cried. And don't picture a single tear dripping down His face. The word John used meant He sobbed. Moreover, the Bible tells us that on another occasion Jesus was so angry He turned over the tables of the moneychangers in the temple (Matthew 21:12ff). And the Apostle John indicates Jesus may have been a little cynical. "Because of the miraculous signs Jesus did in Jerusalem at the Passover celebration, many began to trust in him. But Jesus didn't trust them, because he knew human nature. No one needed to tell him what mankind is really like"—(John 2:23-25). Jesus doesn't seem very joyful. But if we read those stories in context, Jesus' reactions are completely understandable.

Jesus was, after all, human. We would have reacted the same way. His burden to the point of death and sweating blood was because He was about to face the cross in just a matter of hours. It wasn't just the torturous death awaiting Him that shook Him to His core. He was about to take into Himself all the sins of the entire human race. He would absorb sin like a sponge soaking up a disease and then destroy its power by His death and resurrection. I dare say any of us would have called for those 10,000 angels who were waiting in the wings to rescue Him. And when He wept, He was crying at the funeral of His best friend. In America, we hide our grief. It's too awkward to openly express it. We have turned funeral services into celebrations of remembrance for the deceased. In fact, many today are opting out of funerals altogether and having either a brief memorial service or a simple graveside eulogy. We want to push grief away as far as we can. But in Jesus' day, an open display of grief was a sign of respect. They even hired women to wail at funerals. So for Jesus to show great emotion at Lazarus' gravesite was not unusual. It did get everyone's attention, but mostly because Jesus showed up three days late so when He wept, He was alone. And as for His cynicism, the Apostle John didn't intend to cast Jesus as a cynic. Jesus was being realistic, knowing people were following Him because of His miracles, not because of the message He shared.

The Most Joyful Person Who Ever Lived

Jesus was the most joyful person who ever lived. The author to the book of Hebrews, writing about Jesus, quoted a prophecy from the Psalms about the Messiah. "But to the Son he says 'Your throne, O God…'" He interpreted this opening address as referring to Jesus, the Son of God, which is interesting because the Psalmist referred to the Son as being God. "'Therefore, O God, your God has anointed you…'" He called the Messiah God, but then referred to His God. It is an indirect reference to the Trinity. Jesus is God, and the Father is God, and the Holy Spirit is God. But also, the Father is Jesus' God and Jesus is the Father's God and the Holy Spirit is Jesus' and the Father's God and visa versa. The writer was telling us that the Father anointed the Son—God anointed God. " '…Pouring out the oil of joy on you more than on anyone else.'" This is saying the Father anointed Jesus with the joy of the Holy Spirit more than any other person. Jesus is unquestioningly identified as the most joyful person who ever lived.[35]

I never noticed Toyota pickup trucks before. It's not that they weren't there; I just never saw them—that is, until I bought one. Then suddenly, it seemed like everyone drove a Toyota. You probably noticed the same thing when you got your new car. It's the same way with Jesus' joy. If we look for it, we will see it plastered all over the gospels. For example, the gospels tell us children were drawn to Jesus like a magnet. "One day some parents brought their children to Jesus so he could lay his hands on them and pray for them. But the disciples scolded the parents for bothering him. But Jesus said, 'Let the children come to me. Don't stop them! For the Kingdom of Heaven belongs to those who are like these children.' And he placed his hands on their heads and blessed them before he left"—(Matthew 19:13-15). If He were a grouch, children would have avoided Him like the dentist. That was a culture where children were ignored so they would normally not approach anyone outside their family; how much more so if that person was stern, negative or pessimistic. Jesus attracted kids because He was different. He was joyful and kind.

Another thing about Jesus; He liked to crack jokes. Granted, His jokes aren't anything like ours. We are not going to find anywhere in the Gospels where it says, "One day Jesus said, 'A lawyer, a priest and a tax collector walked into a bar…'" You have probably read Jesus' jokes and didn't even realize it. That's because humor changes over time. I was watching an old episode of Bob Hope's comedy routine. He would deliver the punch line and the audience would roll with laughter. But in my house—crickets. I didn't even crack a smile. It just wasn't funny. I am old enough to remember watching Bob Hope live. Back then I thought he was a scream. But humor changes. That's one of the reasons we don't recognize Jesus' humor. Humor in Jesus' day was expressed through exaggerated comparisons. For example, on one occasion when Jesus was teaching, He said, "it is easier for a camel to go through the eye of a needle than for a rich person to enter the Kingdom of God"—(Matthew 19:24). People probably chuckled when they heard those words. That would have been a funny line to a first century Jewish audience. The message Jesus preached was serious, but He couched it in humor. On another occasion, Jesus said, "How can you think of saying, 'Friend, let me help you get rid of that speck in your eye,' when you can't see past the log in your own eye?"—(Luke 6:42). Cue the laugh track. Jesus had a great sense of humor and He knew how to use it in His preaching.

One Christian blogger pointed out something I had never seen before. Luke 10 tells the story of Jesus' 70 disciples returning from an evangelistic tour. He had commissioned them to go preach, heal and cast out demons. When they returned, they expressed their amazement at the authority they had over disease and devils. In verse 18 Jesus responded, "'Yes,' he told them, 'I saw Satan fall from heaven like lightening!'" Then, a few verses later while debriefing with the disciples, Luke wrote, "At that same time Jesus was filled with the joy of the Holy Spirit."[36] Some versions of the Bible say Jesus "rejoiced greatly." The Greek word used in this sentence is made from two syllables; the first means "much;" The second means "jump." Literally it says, "Jesus jump much in the Holy Spirit." Strong's concordance translates it as, "Jump for joy."[37] This year's Super Bowl presented three quarters of boring, and a final quarter of nail biting intensity. Even those who hate the Patriots had to admit it was the most incredible come back in football history. At the end of regulation play, Brady had to execute a two-point conversation to tie the game and send it into overtime. I remember watching that moment and thinking this is it: do or die. Then, incredibly, James White punched it across the goal line. I am sure fans all across New England were glued to their televisions. Everything was library quiet while the play was set up, but the moment White crossed the line, explosions of joy erupted. And I bet people weren't just cheering, but were jumping off their couches, throwing their hands in the air and shouting aloud. That's the picture I see in my mind when Jesus debriefed His disciples. They were recounting their exploits and Jesus literally jumped up and down, shouting for joy, because His salvation plan was working. Satan's kingdom was being destroyed.

Here is one more piece of evidence that reveals the joy of Jesus. Jesus was an extravert. He loved parties. In fact, He compared Himself with His cousin, John, who was the polar opposite. John (the Baptist) lived alone in the desert. He was serious and stern, a fiery prophet. That was exactly what God wanted him to be in order to fulfill his appointed role. Jesus remarked that John was criticized because of his serious disposition, while He was criticized for just the opposite reason. "To what can I compare this generation? It is like children playing a game in the public square. They complain to their friends, 'We played wedding songs, and you didn't dance, so we played funeral songs, and you didn't mourn.' For John didn't spend his time eating and drinking, and you say, 'He's possessed by a demon.' The Son of Man, on the other hand, feasts and drinks, and you say, 'He's a glutton and a drunkard, and a friend of tax collectors and other sinners!' But wisdom is shown to be right by its results"—(Matthew 11:16-19). Jesus didn't conduct Himself like He was at a funeral. Instead, He feasted and drank and had a good time. He hung around what the establishment considered the "wrong kind of people" because He loved them and because they were sick and He had the cure. Jesus was filled with joy and He wanted to give it to His disciples. "I have told you these things so that you will be filled with my joy"—(John 15:11). If Jesus were pessimistic and depressed, His promise would not have motivated His disciples. They would have said, "Ah, no thanks." But it was an effective motivator because His joy was so great.

His Joy Added To Our Joy

Jesus was the most joyful person who ever lived, and He wants to express His joy through us. Just before His arrest, Jesus prayed about the future of His disciples. "Now I am coming to you. I told them many things while I was with them in this world so they would be filled with my joy"—(John 17:13). Jesus died a vicarious death, but He also lived a vicarious life. He lived the perfect life and offers that life to us. He wants to express His life through us, which includes His joy. He wants His joy to impact our relationships. Notice how He promises to include His joy with ours. "I have told you these things so that you will be filled with my joy. Yes, your joy will overflow"—(John 15:11). As wonderful as our joy is, it is incomplete. It reaches its fullness when joined with Jesus' joy. We need His joy flowing through us because there is a difference between His joy and our joy. Our joy is tied to happiness, but His is constant whether we are happy or not. Happiness is connected to circumstances. The word "happiness" comes from the word "hap", which is a root word for "happenstance". We use a form of that word today when we say things like, "Something happened to me." Happiness is connected to what happens to us. Happiness is our emotional response when good things occur. But Jesus' joy goes beyond circumstances. It thrives in spite of circumstances.

Jesus' joy is experienced when we join the Divine Dance. The interplay between the Father, Son and the Holy Spirit is an exchange of perfect love. When we stand in the center of that atmosphere, we experience divine joy. In the heart of that holy storm is the perfect expression of love and joy. As "partakers of the Divine nature" (2 Peter 1:4) we stand in the middle of that wonderful exchange. We are invited into the inner chamber to live in the intimate private quarters of God. The contentment, fulfillment and security that come from that Divine embrace is joy. Such intimacy with God goes beyond circumstances. It lasts forever and cannot be destroyed because it is founded, not on circumstances, but on the eternal nature of God. The Apostle Paul caught a glimpse of it when he wrote, "And I am convinced that nothing can ever separate us from God's love. Neither death nor life, neither angels nor demons, neither our fears for today nor our worries about tomorrow—not even the powers of hell can separate us from God's love"—(Romans 8:38). When we experience Christ's joy, it is contentment in Him, knowing that we are forever in relationship with Him, and not even death can stop it.

When the great reformer, John Wesley, was en route to America to serve as a missionary to the people of Georgia, his ship encountered a life-threatening storm. He and the passengers on board were terrified for their lives; except for a group of Moravian immigrants, that is. During the storm, they worshipped, sang and praised God. Wesley wrote in his journal, "In the midst of the Psalm wherewith their service began, the sea broke over, split the main-sail in pieces, covered the ship and poured in between the decks, as if the great deep had already swallowed us up. A terrible screaming began among the English. The Germans calmly sung on. I asked one of them afterwards; 'Were you not afraid?' He answered, 'I thank God, no.' I asked: 'But were not your women and children afraid?' He replied mildly: 'No, our women and children are not afraid to die.'" The storm was boisterous, but the Moravians kept praising God. Finally, the storm subsided."[38] They had a joy that could not be stopped—the joy of Jesus. It so impressed the young Wesley, that after returning to England he looked up their leader, Peter Boehler and quickly became friends. The Moravian Christians greatly influenced Wesley. That impact eventually led to his conversion experience, and from there was birthed the first great awakening.

Joy Mixed With Sorrow

That doesn't mean we won't ever be sad. The joy of Jesus and human sorrow can coexist in the same heart. Jesus had many times of great sorrow, but His joy actually sustained Him through His sorrow. The author to Hebrews wrote, "Because of the joy awaiting him, he endured the cross"—(Hebrews 12:2a). And what was that joy? It was the anticipation of fully entering into the Divine dance: "Now he is seated in the place of honor beside God's throne"—(12:2b). Joy sustained Him in the midst of sorrow. That, by the way, was more than positive thinking; it was Divine reality. Jesus didn't just hope He would be in heaven with the Father; it was truth. We may have a positive attitude in the midst of trial, but that's not enough. When the Titanic sunk from hitting an iceberg, a group of musicians played on deck, hoping to calm the passengers who were scrambling to get into lifeboats. They continued until their stage permanently dipped beneath the liquid curtain of an icy grave. One passenger wrote, "Many brave things were done that night, but none were more brave than those done by men playing minute after minute as the ship settled quietly lower and lower in the sea. The music they played served alike as their own immortal requiem and their right to be recalled on the scrolls of undying fame."[39] That was a heroic display of optimism. However, we can be optimistic when our Titanic is sinking, but there comes a point when our body hits the frigid water and no matter how positive we are, our breath will be snatched away. Human joy isn't enough when our Titanic is sinking. We need the supernatural fruit of the Spirit. We need the embrace that comes from the Divine dance. Jesus wants to embrace us and pull us into the dance so we can share in His joy. There are a couple of reasons He wants to share His joy with us.

Jesus' Joy And Our Relationships

Not only does it sustain us in struggle, but also the joy of Jesus affects our relationships. Joy is contentment because we stand in the center of the Divine dance. When we are in Christ and He is in us, then we are in relationship with the Father, the Son and the Holy Spirit. That relationship provides us with ultimate acceptance. We are loved, and accepted by God: totally pleasing and completely forgiven. Our lives have purpose, security and significance. Our identity is completed in Him, so that regardless of what others may think of us, God is thrilled with us. If we rest content in His love for us and His assessment of us, then that frees us from the things that can damage relationships. But when we are not in the center of the Divine dance, we are unprotected. We find ourselves searching for a sense of significance: we look for meaning apart from God. We seek acceptance from those around us.

Security, significance and acceptance cannot ultimately come from people, and so the quest to find those things from others leads to all kinds of relationally destructive behaviors—comparing ourselves with others, having to prove ourselves, being worried about what other people will think of us, being the emotional slave of other people, trying to gain their approval, struggles with greed, envy and jealousy. Jesus didn't have any of that in His life. That's why He was free to hang out with children when most people ignored them; to talk to women when that was a social taboo; to touch lepers when people shunned and avoided them and to spend time with those living on the margins of society. He was free to love others because He wasn't trying to make Himself out to be great. In fact, He considered the needs of others more important than His own. He could do that because of joy. He was free to love extravagantly, unhindered by the baggage of a comparative focus. He washed disciples feet when other teachers would have refused to stoop to such a diminished role. He offered to visit a Roman Centurion's home to heal his servant, when any "self-respecting" Jew would have shunned the thought. He allowed a prostitute to wash His feet with her tears, knowing what those around were thinking about Him because of it. He selected disciples the world laughed at. He genuinely could love anyone because of the joy that was His. He was completely contented and fulfilled in His relationship with His Father and had nothing to prove. And because of that, He could freely love others.

Many people are so driven to find meaning and contentment in life by the approval of others; they place themselves in a perfectionistic spiral of destruction. In the early 90's I was certified as a counselor trainer under the auspice of Freedom Ministries. Dr. Ron Miller trained us. I remember him sharing the cycle of destruction. He said that people often try to gain the approval of the significant others in their lives. When they perform well, they feel accepted. When they don't they feel rejected. Often, however, once they reach a certain level of performance, either they or the significant other in their life will raise the bar so that next time the standard of performance will have to be higher in order to gain the same level of approval. Such a cycle creates perfectionism: always reaching for a higher standard, but never quite achieving it. That leads to wide mood swings. A kind of manic-depressive shifting happens each time we succeed or fail to meet our perceived standard. Such a person quickly becomes the emotional slave to the expectations of others. The failure to always reach the expected standard leads to increased frustration levels. That produces impatience, irritability, argumentation, strife, conflict and a short fuse. Such living leads to relationship stress, which results in depleted adrenalin levels. That constant strain leads to anger, bitterness, conflict, rejection, abuse, eventually depression and possibly suicide.[40] It is a destructive downward spiral that plays havoc on relationships. Jesus was so free from all of that baggage that He was able to endure ultimate rejection to the point of dying on the cross for us. And it was His joy that allowed Him to engage in the ultimate expression of rejection. "Because of the joy awaiting him, he endured the cross"—(Hebrews 12:2a).

Identifying The Barriers

It is Jesus' joy that stops the downward spiral. If His joy is free to flow through our lives, then we can be lifted from a pattern of destructive behavior. Because a Christian has the Spirit of Jesus in them, they already possess His joy. But there are barriers that block the joy of Jesus from flowing through our lives. We have to identify those barriers and cast them down so the Lord's joy is free to flow though us. What are those barriers and how do we cast them down? The main culprit is envy. The Apostle Paul identified envy as one of the deeds of the flesh. "Now the deeds of the flesh are evident, which are…envying"—(Galatians 5:19, 21a). We may think the opposite of joy is sadness, but it's not. Jesus was both joyful and sad while praying in Gethsemane. He was so burdened, He literally sweat drops of blood. Yet moments before entering the garden He sang a hymn of celebration with His disciples. Hebrews says it was actually His joy that sustained Him while facing the brutal reality of the cross (Hebrews 12:2).

Envy is the opposite of joy because joy is contentment in Christ: the knowledge that we rest in the center of the Divine dance. However, when we don't feel loved by God, we seek contentment from other sources and that leads to envy. In the spring of the year, when armies went out to fight, King David stayed behind while his army was at war. One night he was on his roof, looking over the surrounding neighborhood. Next-door was the home of Uriah, one of his faithful soldiers. Uriah was away fighting, but his wife, Bathsheba was home. She was taking a bath on her roof. David saw her and wanted her. He had a harem full of women, but he wanted this one. He was trying to satisfy something that was missing in his heart. Envy was at work. He was king, so he could do whatever he wanted. He summoned her to his chambers and slept with her. Later he learned she was pregnant. Adultery was a capitol crime, so he covered it up. Long story short—he had Uriah killed, and then quickly married Bathsheba to make it look like the baby was conceived legitimately. Eventually David was discovered. His prayer of repentance is recorded in Psalm 51. David's envy led to a great explosion of sin, but the cost was the damming of joy in his soul. In his penitential prayer David connected his sin to the absence of joy. "Restore to me the joy of your salvation"—(Psalm 51:12a). We may not think we have a problem with envy, but further examination shows it's more of an issue than we realize. Les Carter, in his book *Mind Over Emotions*, developed a list of questions to reveal our tendency to envy.

1. Do you work extremely hard to come out looking good?
2. Do you examine others with a critical eye?
3. Do you have hidden feelings of inferiority?
4. Do you complain about not getting fair treatment?
5. Do you have an insatiable desire for success?
6. Do you need a lot of recognition for your achievements?
7. Do you tend to be status conscious?
8. Do you find it hard to pay compliments to others?
9. Do you keep score of your own good deeds and those of others?
10. Are you willing to pass along negative rumors about a successful person?
11. Do you put on a false front in order to appear impressive?
12. Do you base your self-image on your performance?[41]

If you answered yes to some of these questions you may have trouble with envy, even though you may not have recognized it. I bet you answered yes to a few, because we all struggle with envy to one degree or another. And envy is a problem because all of those behaviors hurt relationships. Many of the Biblical tragedies stemmed from envy. Cain envied Abel because God accepted Abel's offering and not Cain's, so he killed his brother. Joseph's brothers envied him because he was clearly their father's favorite, so they staged his death and sold him as a slave to a travelling caravan. King Saul envied David because the people celebrated David's defeat of Goliath by minimizing Saul's contribution. They chanted, "Saul killed his thousands, but David his ten thousands"—(1 Samuel 18:7). Saul eventually tried to kill David. Envy consistently led to resentment, suspicion, hatred and murder. Envy is a problem we need to confront, but if we are going to deal with it, we first need to know the things that cause envy.

Two Common Causes of Envy

The first trigger that leads to envy is living with a comparative focus. People are constantly comparing themselves with others. We do it all the time. Like when the Patriots won this year's Super Bowl, immediately people were comparing Brady to others saying he is the best quarterback of all time—although that is true. (Don't get mad at me. That's just the facts.) Seriously though, we do this in our own lives, comparing ourselves with those around us. We even do it in the church. The Apostle Paul was quick to deal with the issue. "For we are not bold to class or compare ourselves with some of those who commend themselves; but when they measure themselves by themselves and compare themselves with themselves, they are without understanding"—(2 Corinthians 10:12). It's true that some are better at certain things than we are, but the problem is, we translate that into saying someone is a better person than we are. It is so easy to look at someone else's job, home, good looks, or education and use those things to draw conclusions about our own shortcomings. A comparative focus tends to place us in a competition, where if someone else wins, we think we automatically have to lose. But their success does not stop ours, nor does it mean they are more valuable than we are. Possessing more valuables does not make us more valuable. But when we compare ourselves to them, it triggers envy.

The second trigger that leads to envy is being overly concerned with personal rights. It starts when we are young. "He got more Christmas presents than me." "She got the last piece of cake." "It's not fair." This extends into adulthood and blossoms into envy. The book of 1 Kings tells a gruesome story of envy at its worst. "Some time later two prostitutes came to the king to have an argument settled. 'Please, my lord,' one of them began, 'this woman and I live in the same house. I gave birth to a baby while she was with me in the house. Three days later this woman also had a baby. We were alone; there were only two of us in the house. But her baby died during the night when she rolled over on it. Then she got up in the night and took my son from beside me while I was asleep. She laid her dead child in my arms and took mine to sleep beside her. And in the morning when I tried to nurse my son, he was dead! But when I looked more closely in the morning light, I saw that it wasn't my son at all.' Then the other woman interrupted, 'It certainly was your son, and the living child is mine.' 'No,' the first woman said, 'the living child is mine, and the dead one is yours.' And so they argued back and forth before the king. Then the king said, 'Let's get the facts straight. Both of you claim the living child is yours, and each says that the dead one belongs to the other. All right, bring me a sword.' So a sword was brought to the king. Then he said, 'Cut the living child in two, and give half to one woman and half to the other!' Then the woman who was the real mother of the living child, and who loved him very much, cried out, 'Oh no, my lord! Give her the child—please do not kill him!' But the other woman said, 'All right, he will be neither yours nor mine; divide him between us!' Then the king said, 'Do not kill the child, but give him to the woman who wants him to live, for she is his mother!' When all Israel heard the king's decision, the people were in awe of the king, for they saw the wisdom God had given him for rendering justice"—(1 Kings 3:16-28).

The Bible says we are to lay down our rights. "Then Jesus said to His disciples, 'If anyone wishes to come after me, he must deny himself"—(Matthew 16:24a). "Whoever slaps you on your right cheek, turn the other to him also"—(Matthew 5:39b). "If anyone wants to sue you and take your shirt, let him have your coat also. Whoever forces you to go one mile, go with him two"—(Matthew 5:40-41). "Actually, then, it is already a defeat for you, that you have lawsuits with one another. Why not rather be wronged? Why not rather be defrauded"—(1 Corinthians 6:7). "Have this attitude in yourselves which was also in Christ Jesus, who, although He existed in the form of God, did not regard equality with God a thing to be grasped, but emptied Himself, taking the form of a bond-servant"—(Philippians 2:5-7a). This is all about laying down our personal rights. As long as we cling tightly to them, our heart is fertile soil for envy to grow.

5 Steps to Stopping the Green Monster

There are several steps we can take to deal with envy. If you are meeting with a disciple, these steps can form practical exercises to work through with your disciple. At the end of this chapter we will look at how to set goals around these steps to deal with envy. If we can deny this aberration of self, then it will leave room for joy to flow through our lives.

1. The first step to dealing with envy is to live by God's definition of success. So many focus on success being about achievements, possessions and status. I like how the poet Maya Angelou defined success. She said, "Success is liking yourself, liking what you do, and liking how you do it."[42] Whatever our definition, as a Christian, success in life needs to be attached to the purposes of God. A good question to focus on and try to answer is: In what ways are you wired to best glorify God and love others? I know a retired woman; I'll call her Sarah, who has found a way to use her talents to encourage others. Sarah enjoys making homemade greeting cards. But these aren't just a few scribbles on a folded piece of cardboard. No. Sarah creates intricate, elaborate works of art that are tailor fit to an individual's specific situation. On many occasions, my wife, Marcia, and I have received a card from Sarah that was not only beautiful, but said the exact thing we needed to hear at that moment. Sarah sends her cards to people all over the country. She demonstrates great love and concern for others by using her talents to brighten someone's life. That's how Sarah glorifies God and loves others. What talents or gifts do you possess? How could you use that gift to encourage or express love to other people? If we spend our lives showing others love in the way we best can do it, our lives will be successful, for it's in loving others in our unique way that brings glory to God. If we can focus on that, then our eyes will be off others and trained on God and His purposes. If we are walking by faith in the center of God's will, then that is a successful life.

2. We must focus on the real source of our envy. If we are envious of another person, it is important to release them from blame. Regardless of what we may feel about them, it is not their fault. They do not control our feelings. If we look beneath the surface, we may discover the real reason we feel envious toward another person has little to do with that individual and their possessions or accomplishments. On further investigation, we may find it has more to

do with our own heart. The feelings of envy are not because they have something we lack. Someone else having what we want doesn't keep us from having what we want. The feelings of envy are because we have made the object of our desire an idol. "Therefore consider the members of your earthly body as dead to immorality, impurity, passion, evil desire, and greed, which amounts to idolatry"—(Colossians 3:5). Separating the source of our feelings from the individual toward whom we feel them makes it possible to be happy for them. It also allows us to realize we are dealing, not with the fact that we lack something, but instead, the fact that we have an idol in our heart. Thus, we need to repent. Envy hides in the dark recesses of our heart. That which stays in the dark has power over us. When we confess our envy and repent of it, it weakens its power over us. However, we have to confess it to another person. James tells us we are to confess our sins. But notice he says we are to confess them to one another. "Confess your sins to each other and pray for each other so that you may be healed"—(James 5:16). The confession to one another is not so we can be forgiven. God has already forgiven us in Christ. The confession is so we can be healed. Many years ago I sat with a spiritual advisor and poured out my heart. I had harbored hatred toward someone and it had stymied my spiritual growth. I was stuck. I had confessed my sin to God many times, but never seemed to get anywhere. I knew God had forgiven me, but there wasn't any kind of release. But when I confessed my sin to God in the presence of another person, it was humbling. Though God was the One I needed to be most concerned about, it was easy to confess to Him. He knows everything about me even before I confess. There isn't any risk in sharing with God my innermost thoughts. He is aware of all of them before I am. But to pour out my heart to God in front of another person is a different story. I was unmasked. It was difficult, but when I did it, something broke open inside of me. I broke into a torrent of tears. I sobbed aloud for minutes. During that time, a wave of healing rushed over my soul. I walked out of that room a different man. When we confess our envy to God in the presence of another, its power over us is broken.

3. We need to express gratitude. This is a practical way to help us deal with our feelings of envy. When we find our minds drifting to

the realm of what we don't have, we must make a conscious effort to think about what we do have. "Be anxious for nothing, but in everything by prayer and supplication with thanksgiving let your requests be made known to God"—(Philippians 4:6). Notice, Paul says that when we pray for things, we do so with thanksgiving. "And give thanks for everything to God the Father in the name of our Lord Jesus Christ"—(Ephesians 5:20). Being grateful is a lot like being mindful. It's about focusing on the present and turning our thoughts to what is already good in our life, instead of thinking about what is lacking. Here are some practical ways to do that:

First, start by writing a list of the things you are grateful for. We may be able to think of two or three, but to come up with a list of 25 things can be difficult. Our minds are often in a rut of complaint. We can easily think of the things that irritate or disappoint us. But to focus on the positive blessings of life cuts against the grain. But do it. It is a great exercise to shift our minds in the right direction. Here are some prompters that may help get you started. Write down some of your abilities or talents. What things can you do that you are pretty good at? Who is your best friend? What qualities about them make them special to you? What are the kinds of foods you enjoy eating? When is the last time you had a huge belly laugh? What are the kinds of things that make you laugh? What memories can you recall that bring a smile to your face? Are there any plans, events or trips on your calendar to which you are looking forward? Of all the things you own, what is most precious to you? What accomplishments have you achieved that you had to work toward? As you think in those categories, ideas will come to mind. List them, and then thank God for each one. Those are blessings He ultimately brought into your life. It will be helpful to take a couple items and make them a matter of prayer each day. As you think of more, add them to your list. In time you will train yourself to look at life through a grid of gratitude.

Second, try focusing only on positive things for a day. Don't allow yourself one complaint. One thing this exercise will do, is reveal just how negative we can easily become. It is easy to launch into a monologue before even realizing what we are doing. All complaining is off limits. You cannot cut yourself down, or compare yourself unfavorably to someone else, nor wish things in your life were different.[43]

Finally, try saying table grace in a new way. If yours is a family that prays before eating, try this variation. Instead of simply thanking God for the food, go around the table and ask each person to share one thing they are thankful for that happened to them that day. It can be something little, but work to think of one good thing; even if it is only that you were able to get out of bed with breath in your lungs. Think of something. If you do this every night your family shares a meal, it will get you and yours to begin looking through the day for something good for which to thank God.

4. Intentionally compliment others. Think about those in your life toward whom you tend to be envious. What is it about them you wish you had? Perhaps it is a friend who has a much higher paying job than you do. What kind of individual does he/she have to be to hold such a job? What qualities do they possess that make them good at their job? What kind of a person would his or her employer be looking for to hire someone for that position? After thinking through those answers, make it a point to deliberately compliment them for those qualities. Taking the time to think about what you really like about people, and then expressing that out loud, will help your mind stay in a positive place. You won't be as worried about comparing yourself to others.[44]

5. Stay away from complainers because it fosters envy. If our friends are the type to constantly compare jobs, partners and kids, complain about what they don't have and cut down people who do, we might want to start spending time with different people. The goal might be to stay away from negative input for a week. "Negative input" means anything that feeds your envy and makes you wish for something you don't or can't have.[45]

Setting Smart Goals

These exercises are different tasks you can work on with your discipleship partner. They are practical guides to help you focus on your envy and to begin living in a different way. You may want to pick just one exercise and work on that for a week. Take several weeks to work through the list. When working through something like this, however, it is important to set some specific goals. Life coaches call them S.M.A.R.T. goals. Setting a smart goal will help you and your discipleship partner make forward progress. Each letter stands for a different qualifier. S means the goal must be specific. So to say, "Next week I will be a more positive person," is too vague. How are you going to be positive? You might say, "Next week I am going to genuinely compliment five people." M stands for measurable. How do you know you accomplished your goal if it is not measureable? To say, "I am going to compliment some people," is hard to measure. When are you going to do it? How many are you going to compliment? The letter A stands for achievable. The goal can't be idealistic, or impossible. To say you are going to compliment 30 people next week may be too ambitious. To narrow that down to one person a day is more achievable. R stands for results based. That means the goal must be something you can physically do. To "be a more positive person", doesn't speak about something you do, but rather something you are. That cannot be a goal. You have to ask how you are going to be a more positive person in order to create a goal that is results based. T stands for time bound. There must be a time limit set to the goal, or it will never get accomplished. To put all that together, a smart goal might be: "Next week I am going to genuinely complement five different people—one person for each day of the work week. I am going to compliment them to their face about something I admire in them. I will complete that goal before we meet next Saturday. That will give you and your disciple measurable things to work on in the effort to fight off envy. Then, when you come together, you can talk about your progress. How did you do on your goal? What did you learn from the experience? What observations did you make about yourself? How difficult was it? What about it was difficult and why? How do you think God might want you to grow in this area?

If you genuinely work on these steps in a discipleship context over a period of time, you will begin to experience the joy of Jesus flowing through your life. When we can genuinely be happy for other people's successes, and when we can be secure in God's love and acceptance of us, then the joy of Jesus will flow through our hearts.

6
Shalom

Our world is in a constant state of war. War is defined as an active conflict that has claimed more than 1,000 lives. Of the past 3,400 years of recorded history, there has been a war going on for all but 268 of them. We have been at war for 92% of human history.[46] The story of our own country closely reflects that of the world since our founding in 1776. We have been at war during 220 of our 241 years. There are only 21 calendar years in which the U.S. has not engaged in any wars. That means we have been at war 91% of the time. No U.S. President truly qualifies as a peacetime President. Instead, all U.S. Presidents can technically be considered "war Presidents." The U.S. has never gone a decade without war. The only time the U.S. went five years without war was 1935-1940.[47] Our world has always been at war, yet people cry for peace. The United Nations was created to put an end to war, but it hasn't helped. The only way peace will come is when Jesus Christ rules this world. When He came into the world the first time, He came as the Prince of Peace (Isaiah 9:6). When He came, He did bring peace, but not the kind the world was looking for. Jesus said, "Peace I leave with you; my peace I give to you; not as the world gives do I give to you"—(John 14:27). When Jesus speaks of peace He is talking about Shalom, the presence of serenity and tranquility. He offers wholeness, completeness and soundness of heart and mind.

When Jesus promised us peace He did not mean He would stop all wars. In fact, He bluntly stated that wars would be fought because of Him. "Don't imagine that I came to bring peace to the earth! I came not to bring peace, but a sword. I have come to set a man against his father, a daughter against her mother, and a daughter-in-law against her mother-in-law. Your enemies will be right in your own household"—(Matthew 10:34-36). Don't misunderstand, Jesus did not come to make families fight, but He did recognize people would, because following Jesus is offensive. So Jesus offered peace in the middle of conflict. Paul characterized it this way, "The peace of God, which surpasses all comprehension, will guard your hearts and your minds in Christ Jesus"—(Philippians 4:7). This peace goes beyond human comprehension. It doesn't make earthly sense, because it thrives in the midst of chaos. Jesus endured unimaginable stress during His final meeting with His disciples. They shared the Passover meal together in an upper room. Jesus knew He would be arrested, tortured and killed in a matter of hours, yet He functioned with a total sense of peace. He told His disciples He had been looking forward to their meal and was genuinely happy to share it with them. There was no sense of dread. They knew something was wrong, and instead of commiserating with them, Jesus encouraged them. "Don't let your hearts be troubled. Trust in God, and trust also in me"—(John 14:1). After the meal they sang a hymn of worship. When Jesus prayed in Gethsemane He was under such duress He literally sweat drops of blood. Yet after praying three hours, He walked out from His prayer closet with a total sense of Shalom. In fact, when the arresting mob entered the garden He didn't wait for them to find Him, but He approached them. When Peter drew a dagger to fight, Jesus rebuked him and told him to put his weapon away. When the Temple leaders told the Lord they were looking for Jesus of Nazareth, He responded by saying, "I am." That statement was the same language God used when Moses asked the Lord of the burning bush His name. Jesus identified Himself with the burning bush, with Jehovah. When He uttered those words the entire group fell backwards to the ground. One statement from Jesus' lips was enough to knock an entire battery of soldiers and officials to the ground. When they got back up, Jesus allowed them to arrest Him. He was demonstrating that He was going willingly. They were not taking Him by force. He was totally composed and marched to His death with complete Shalom. When we are under pressure; when our world is in chaos; when our lives are turned upside-down; when war is raging around us and within us, Jesus offers Shalom.

Satanic Opposition

Satan has no interest in us being in any kind of calm state. He wants our emotions to blow up. He attacks us to try and stop the peace of Jesus from ruling our hearts. One of his greatest weapons to destroy our peace is anxiety. The enemy hits us with anxiety to stop the flow of

Jesus' peace. If we are going to experience the inner Shalom of Jesus, if we are going to inject Jesus' peace into our relationships, we have to deal with anxiety. Anxiety is to emotional peace what war is to national peace. It is a huge problem. More than 1 in 5 Americans take medications for anxiety or depression, ranging from things like Prozac to Xanax. That's 20% of Americans, which is a 22% increase since 2001.[48] I understand why people are getting anxious. According to David Powlison, Satan seeks to fill us with fear, and there are a lot of things to be anxious about. Death is a fact of life. "No matter how pleasant our lives are, some very big, bad news is waiting at the end: Each of us will die. Everyone we love will die. Death is the source of very intense anxiety for almost everyone. This anxiety fuels our fears, not only about our death, but also about our health and the health of those we love. Relationships don't last. Relationships are also a huge source of anxiety. We value relationships, but they change and sometimes break apart; a spouse dies, a marriage fails, children leave home, and friends drift away or even turn on us. We fear the loneliness, the loss, the hurt, and the betrayal that comes with broken relationships. We don't have enough money. Most of us worry about money. We can't escape this anxiety. It touches every part of our lives. Money worries are tied to so many things: security, identity, status. Each can be affected by how much money we have or don't have."[49]

Panic Attacks

I am not speaking as someone who doesn't understand the struggles people have with anxiety, nor am I in anyway criticizing those who take anti-anxiety drugs. Drugs are like scaffolding on a building. In order to repair a building it is often necessary to erect scaffolding. It is a temporary structure. It does not fix the problem, but makes it possible for the problem to be fixed. Medication is the same way. I have taken anti-anxiety medication in the past. I only took it for a season, but it helped me gain some sense of balance to enable me to focus on the things that needed permanent adjustment. I awoke from a deep sleep one night with clammy skin and searing pain in my chest and down my arm. I was sure I was having a heart attack. It was the middle of the night and I didn't want to wake my wife, so I drove myself to the hospital. (I know, that was stupid. Believe me, I heard about it later!). I was calm, but in pain. I arrived at the emergency and nonchalantly told the receptionist I thought I was having a heart attack. I discovered when you say those words everything stops. No forms to fill; no sitting in the waiting room—you are immediately put to the front of the line and rushed to care! How different from when I crawled into the emergency room one time with a kidney stone. I was writhing in pain and could hardly talk. When the nurse handed me a pen and told me to fill out some forms, my hand shook so much I could hardly write. I was clearly in great distress. Her reply? Wait over there until someone can see you. Next time you are in the hospital with a kidney stone, tell them you have pain in your chest as well. That will get you to the front of the line where you can get those wonderful drugs that take that horrible pain away. Just kidding…sort of. I digress. Back to my heart attack—turns out, it was only stress. I didn't think I was under any stress, but my body said differently. I have had panic attacks since then. They are nothing to joke about. They are real, and terrifying. If you have ever experienced one, you know how horrible they can be. I understand what it is like for those who struggle with anxiety.

Medication Has Its Place

I am going to share with you the Bible's method for dealing with anxiety, however, I don't want to oversell this and say if you take these specific steps, all anxiety will go and you can drop your medication. Pain is the body's alarm system telling us there is a problem. Let's say our stomach hurts so we take a Tylenol. That drug will tell the brain to stop registering the pain. It brings immediate relief, but the thing that was causing the pain is still there. We need to go to a doctor to deal with the source of the problem. Anxiety medication is the same thing. When we are in emotional pain, we may take a drug that will immediately relieve the pain, but the problem is still there. The drug does not take away the cause of the pain, only the feeling of the pain. The surgery that needs to be done to deal with the cause of the emotional pain is through Christ. I am going to share with you how He brings His peace into our lives to deal with the pain of anxiety. Let's think about it this way: you're driving down the road and "Bam!" you blow a tire. You have to get out and change it. It could be because you ran over a nail, but let's say it's because your treads wore too thin. You had an emergency and so you took out the spare and fixed it. But the problem was, you never did any preventative maintenance. If you had checked the tread on your tires every now and then, if you had rotated them and kept them balanced, then you could have seen an issue developing and taken steps to fix it before you had a flat. Taking medication is like using the spare. When in a crisis, it is a necessary help. Living in the peace of Christ is like practicing consistent maintenance. You can see a problem coming and you are prepared to handle it. That doesn't mean you still won't have emergencies. I am consistent on my vehicle maintenance, but I recently hit a nail and so still had to use my spare, despite my religious adherence to vehicle maintenance check ups. There will still be crises where we need medical help to deal with things, even when we are experiencing the peace of Christ. But when we live in the peace of Christ, we are more consistently in a state of Shalom. That is essential to navigating the stressful currents of human relationships. But even when we do have a blown tire on the road, the peace of Christ is there to assist. The Bible is clear about our part in dealing with anxiety so Christ's peace can flow through our lives.

Prayer and Focus

Paul's prescription for anxiety is found in his letter to the Philippians. "Be anxious for nothing, but in everything by prayer and supplication with thanksgiving let your requests be made known to God. And the peace of God, which surpasses all comprehension, will guard your hearts and your minds in Christ Jesus. Finally, brethren, whatever is true, whatever is honorable, whatever is right, whatever is pure, whatever is lovely, whatever is of good repute, if there is any excellence and if anything worthy of praise, dwell on these things. The things you have learned and received and heard and seen in me, practice these things, and the God of peace will be with you"—

(Philippians 4:6-9). Notice the very first phrase in this passage; "Be anxious for nothing, but in everything." There is a contrast between nothing and everything. They are Polar opposites. Nothing means "not one thing." Everything means "every single thing." Paul is saying, when we encounter situations, there is something we should never do, and something we should always do. And because the word "everything" is the opposite of the word "nothing", it is an indication to us that when in anxious moments, we are to do the exact opposite of worry. What is the opposite of worry? If we picture a nervous person as the worrier, than we may see the opposite of that as one who is confident. But that is misleading. The opposite of worry is not confidence. According to Paul, the opposite of worry is prayer, supplication and thanksgiving. "But in everything by prayer and supplication with thanksgiving let your requests be made known to God"—(Philippians 4:6).

There are three activities Paul instructed us to do to fight anxiety. The first is prayer. The word Paul used means adoration and worship. This is vital because the first thing we must not do, is launch into our wish list and ask God to deal with our situations. First we have to worship Him. That, by the way, is an indication Paul was referring to more than an emergency response when a tire blows out. When the crisis occurs, we are not in much of a frame of mind to worship. This is referring to an activity that would be a regular part of our life. When we go before God, we do not start with our problems, we start with God. It honors God, but more than that, it reminds us of who He is. Our problem can seem so big in our eyes that we need to be reminded God is bigger. The next word Paul used, was supplication. This refers to the specific things we want from God. We start with praising God, and then we are ready to make our requests. Paul wrapped it up with the word thanksgiving. When making requests to God, we must keep a grateful heart. It is easy to get so bogged down in our trouble that we become ungrateful and lose hope. We thank God for what He has already done in our lives. He has saved us, called us, provided for us many times over. Such gratitude keeps us in a humble spirit and builds our faith. These three things are how Paul said we make our requests to God. When we do that, Paul told us the results in verse 7. "And the peace of God, which surpasses all comprehension, shall guard your hearts and your minds in Christ Jesus." The word, "guard" is a military word that means to garrison. God's peace will protect our emotions and thoughts. This is an important activity, but there is more we have to do. We also have to focus our thinking.

"Finally, brethren, whatever is true, whatever is honorable, whatever is right, whatever is pure, whatever is lovely, whatever is of good repute, if there is any excellence and if anything worthy of praise, let your mind dwell on these things"—(Philippians 4:8). It is important where we allow our minds to dwell. Paul was encouraging us to focus on things that are accurate, sincere, true, holy, just, clean, gracious and good. The list is self-explanatory, but the point is, how we think is all-important. Sin attacks our thinking. Paul said in Romans, "But I see a different law in the members of my body, waging war against the law of my mind, and making me a prisoner of the law of sin which is in my members"—(Romans 7:23). There is a principle of evil that continually attacks the mind. When the mind dwells on earthly things, death results. Notice the contrast with peace. "For the mind set on the flesh is death, but the mind set on the Spirit is life and peace"—(Romans 8:6). So the first thing we do to help us deal with anxiety is prayer and mental focus.

Humility and Community

Paul was describing a lifestyle, not an emergency response. These activities are important to put us in a state of Shalom so we are in a right frame of mind to deal with issues when they arise. This isn't a quick fix. It is a long-term strategy. That becomes clearer when we look at the next step to dealing with anxiety. This time we will listen to the teaching of Saint Peter. "So humble yourselves under the mighty power of God, and at the right time he will lift you up in honor. Give all your worries and cares to God, for he cares about you. Stay alert! Watch out for your great enemy, the devil. He prowls around like a roaring lion, looking for someone to devour"—(1 Peter 5:6-8). Some think we deal with anxiety by being strong, but God says the way to deal with it is to be humble. The phrase "humble yourselves" is in the imperative voice. That means it's a command. It is something we are expected to do. We make the choice to humble ourselves. It is important we are clear about what it means to humble ourselves. It does not mean to look down on your self. To focus on how low or inept we are, is actually a disguised form of pride. We may not be arrogant, but the focus is still on self. Humility isn't thinking poorly of your self, but rather, not thinking of your self at all. I believe there are three ways humility needs to be expressed.

1. Dependence on God. The height of arrogance is to live life without God. The person who believes they don't need God—that they can make it on their own without His help—is arrogant. This is one of the reasons prayer is so important. It keeps us in touch with our need for God. When Jesus taught the disciples how to pray, He offered them a formula for prayer. The "Lord's Prayer" is really an outline for the things Jesus considered important to pray about. One of the lines says, "Give us this day our daily bread." Jesus instructed the disciples to pray daily for their sustenance. This prayer was intended for all believers for all time. Those of us who are blessed enough to live in America have plenty of daily bread. In fact, we don't need to ask God to give us our daily bread, for it is sitting in our refrigerators right now. In Jesus' day, it wasn't guaranteed they would have bread to eat on any given day. There are many around the world who are today in that same situation, but not here in America. Most of us will eat ourselves to death, rather than starve to death. So technically speaking, we don't need to pray and ask for the food we need to eat today. Yet, Jesus instructed us to do so. The reason, it keeps us in touch with our need for God. We may have food in the cupboard because we bought groceries last Saturday. We may have groceries because we earn a paycheck. We may have a paycheck because we have a job. We may have gotten that job because we were educated and interviewed well. But who gives us the strength to get up every morning? Who gave us the intelligence to learn in school? Who gives us breath and life? Ultimately it all comes from God. Jesus wanted to keep us in touch with that reality. We pray for daily bread because we know behind all our abilities and opportunities is the generous hand of God. Jesus instructed His disciples to pray that daily because He wanted them to live in a continuous state of

dependence on God. Though we live in a land of prosperity, we humble ourselves by remembering that all our blessings come from God. Prayer is a discipline that helps keep that reality in check.

2. Proper interdependence on others. One of my weaknesses is I don't like to ask others for help. I feel like I am putting them out. I like it when others ask me for help. I feel very blessed to assist a friend, but somehow I don't feel the same way when I need them to help me. It's really another form of pride. I have to learn to get over it. But I have found that many others feel the same way. People are reluctant to ask others for help. My wife worked for a government agency that provided heating assistance to the needy. She had to conduct interviews with prospective clients. We lived in Maine where winters get routinely below zero. Heating is a matter of survival, not just comfort. She noticed the people who really needed help were often the elderly. Yet, they were the ones who would never think of asking for assistance. They grew up in a culture where it was expected you fend for yourself. There were no government handouts. As a pastor, I have noticed the same thing. Our elderly do not easily ask others for help. It's a point of dignity. I get it. I feel the same way. But the church was expected to live in community. We often interpret the Bible through the lens of rugged individualism. We read Paul's admonitions as if they were speaking to the individual. But almost every one of the commands in the New Testament were written to the group. They are to be carried out in community. There is no place for a solo expression of the faith in Christianity. That means we are our brother's keeper. We are responsible for one another. We are expected to be involved in each other's lives. Thus, we are to live in interdependence on one another; helping each other, supporting each other, holding each other accountable. When you are hurting, are you willing to share your hurt with others? When you need help, do you hide it from others? Do you let others know you need prayer? Are you willing to let others minister to you? Or are you like Peter who didn't want Jesus to wash his feet? Jesus told Peter if he didn't allow Him to wash his feet, then Jesus would have nothing to do with Peter (John 13:8). Peter responded by telling the Lord to give him a bath. I love it. He was an all-or-nothing kind of guy. We don't need to give each other baths, but a little foot

washing wouldn't hurt.

   3. Humility means we are not going to promote self. We do not need to get the applause. We are not interested in making sure we look good. We are interested in building up the body of Christ. In verse 6, Peter wrote, "Humble yourselves, therefore, under the mighty hand of God, that He may exalt you at the proper time." The word "therefore" connects us back to the previous verse. It puts us in touch with the central promise of this passage—"God is opposed to the proud, but gives grace to the humble. Humble yourselves therefore" (vs.5-6a). That statement "God opposes the proud, but gives grace to the humble" explains how this works. When we are attacked by anxiety, we need God's rescue—His peace to guard our hearts and minds. But God responds in one of two ways, depending on whether we are humble or proud. It says that God opposes the proud. When Satan attacks a proud person with anxiety, God does not protect their heart and mind. When we think of a proud person we may assume it is an arrogant person. It may include arrogance, but it goes much deeper than that. The proud person is the independent, stubborn person. God opposes people who are this way because they refuse to let Him work in their life. They will handle life on their own terms. Therefore they are open to the enemy's attacks. Notice verse 8 says, "Be of sober spirit, be on the alert. Your adversary, the devil, prowls about like a roaring lion, seeking someone to devour." The context of this passage makes it clear the attack Peter is speaking about is anxiety. "Give all your worries and cares to God, for he cares about you. Stay alert! Watch out for your great enemy, the devil. He prowls around like a roaring lion, looking for someone to devour"—(1 Peter 5:7-8). He is a roaring lion, but he has no teeth. Those were pulled at the cross. He devours with his roar. The lion's roar is to illicit fear. That's what Satan tries to do to us. But notice Peter said that God gives grace to the humble. "God is opposed to the proud, but gives grace to the humble"—(v.5). Grace is God's presence in our lives to empower us to live out His will. If we live in community, and dependency on God, and pray for everything, we can be ready when anxiety attacks. That will bring calm to our relationships. Jesus lived this way every moment. He was the most peaceful person who ever lived, even though conflict and

opposition constantly surrounded Him. He wants His peace to flow through us.

Questions and Goals

Discuss the following questions with your discipleship leader / or group. Then, based on your answers, write some S.M.A.R.T. goals on which to work. Remember a smart goal is one that is specific, measurable, achievable, realistic and time-stamped. Then hold one another accountable to reach your goals.

- In what ways do you see anxiety in your life?

- Can you identify your common triggers for anxiety?

- When you encounter anxious moments do you tend to default to prayer or something else? If not prayer, what else?

- Do you have a regular, consistent prayer time?

- When you pause to spend a few minutes in prayer, do you begin with praise and worship, or do you tend to jump right into your requests?

- Do you practice any type of meditation where you focus your mind on positive things?

- Do you easily ask others for help?

- When others talk to you about stressful situations, do you find yourself thinking about how that affects them, or how it affects you?

7
Root Causes

A study of the fruit of the Spirit is really a study of the life of Jesus. Jesus epitomizes each characteristic to the ultimate degree. The first fruit is love because Jesus is love. But not only is He love, but He is the most loving person who has ever lived. And so it is with all the fruit. Jesus was the most joyful person who ever lived. Same with peace; He was the most peaceful person. And likewise with patience— Jesus is the most patient person who ever lived, and He wants His patience to flow through us. This is good news because so many will confess to not being very patient. But Jesus doesn't want us to be patient. He wants us to allow Him, who is the ultimate expression of patience, to manifest Himself through us into our relationships.

The Patience of Jesus

The patience of Jesus is easy to see in Scripture. Jesus was trying to prepare His disciples for what would happen when He was arrested. He warned they would flee, but Peter kept insisting he would stay true, even if it meant his death. Jesus went so far as to let Peter know that after he failed, he would return to the Lord. "'But I have pleaded in prayer for you, Simon, that your faith should not fail. So when you have repented and turned to me again, strengthen your brothers.' Peter said, 'Lord, I am ready to go to prison with you, and even to die with you.' But Jesus said, 'Peter, let me tell you something. Before the rooster crows tomorrow morning, you will deny three times that you even know me'"—(Luke 22:32-34). Jesus knew Peter would mess up, and yet He still wanted to use Peter. He even told Peter He wanted him to strengthen his brothers. After Peter denied the Lord and ran away; after Jesus was crucified and buried; after Jesus rose from the dead; Peter was missing in action, broken-hearted, disillusioned, embarrassed and far from the Lord. It would have been so easy to drop him. He rejected Jesus. When Peter denied Jesus, he wasn't just afraid of the village girl, but he outright rejected Jesus because Jesus wasn't the kind of Messiah he thought Jesus should be. He wanted Jesus to defeat the Romans. And when he realized that was not what Jesus came to do, he walked away. Had I been over the group, I would have walked away from Peter. "You rejected me, then fine! I am done with you. I will find someone else!" But that's not what Jesus did. He made sure His angel gave instructions specifically for Peter. The women came to the empty tomb and met an angel, and here is what the angel said: "Now go and tell his disciples, **including Peter**, that Jesus is going ahead of you to Galilee. You will see him there, just as he told you before he died"—(Mark 16:7 emphasis added).

On another occasion when Jesus wanted His disciples to feed 5000 men, plus women and children, the disciples panicked, not knowing how they were going to feed such a large crowd. But Jesus calmly instructed them to have the people sit in groups of 50 and then miraculously fed them all with a couple of fish. Not long after that they were there again with 4000 and the disciples asked the same questions, but Jesus patiently fed them all as well. Shortly after, they were travelling by boat across the Sea of Galilee, and Jesus made a statement about leaven. He was talking about the corrupt influences of the Pharisees, but the disciples thought He was talking about bread. At that moment, they realized they hadn't brought any bread with them for the journey. They panicked, thinking Jesus was upset with them for their lack of preparation. Jesus had recently fed over 9000 people on two separate occasions with a little bread and fish. A lack of bread in the boat was not the problem. These guys weren't getting it. And you would think Jesus would give up. And indeed, you can see He actually is a little frustrated. "But the disciples had forgotten to bring any food. They had only one loaf of bread with them in the boat. As they were crossing the lake, Jesus warned them, "Watch out! Beware of the yeast of the Pharisees and of Herod." At this they began to argue with each other because they hadn't brought any bread. Jesus knew what they were saying, so he said, "Why are you arguing about having no bread? Don't you know or understand even yet? Are your hearts too hard to take it in? 'You have eyes—can't you see? You have ears—can't you hear?' Don't you remember anything at all? When I fed the 5,000 with five loaves of bread, how many baskets of leftovers did you pick up afterward?" "Twelve," they said. "And when I fed the 4,000 with seven loaves, how many large baskets of leftovers did you pick up?" "Seven," they said. "Don't you understand yet?" he asked them—(Mark 8:14-21). Jesus was frustrated at their lack of insight. They were so slow to pick up on the truths He wanted them to catch, but even so, He patiently took them to Caesarea Philippi and there taught them about His true identity to help them with their misunderstandings.

There is a cave at the base of the mountain in Caesarea. Its walls are covered with inscriptions to many different gods. It was thought in ancient days that the opening was the gateway to Hades. It is believed this is where Jesus stood with His disciples when He asked them, "Who do people say I am?" They gave various answers—Moses, a prophet, Elijah, etc. But then Jesus asked them directly, "Who do you say I am?" Peter answered, "You are the Christ. The Son of the living God." Jesus blessed him and acknowledged his words were accurate. Then He said He would build His kingdom upon the foundation of Peter's confession (Matthew 16:13-16, Mark 8:27-30, Luke 9:18-21). Here is the God of the universe trying to teach simple fishermen how to walk in supernatural things, but they are too slow to get it. Even so, He continued to work with them and teach them about the Kingdom of God.

On one occasion they were trying to cast a demon out of a boy, but no matter how hard they tried, they could not do it. Finally they came to Jesus frustrated because they could not cast the demon out. "Jesus said to them, 'You faithless people! How long must I be with you? How long must I put up with you? Bring the boy to me'"—(Mark 9:19). You can pick up on the growing frustration, but in the end, Jesus' patience won out. He healed the boy and then took the disciples aside and taught them why they had such trouble casting the demon out.

As I write these words I think how grateful I am that Jesus is like that. How many times have I frustrated the Lord? Sometimes I am so spiritually dull, or I make the same mistakes over and over again. But Jesus patiently walks with me in spite of my many failures. He said He would never leave us for forsake us. It is a comfort to know my foolishness is not more powerful than His resolve. Jesus is the most patient person who ever lived and He wants that same patience operating in and through our lives. In fact, patience is listed as one of the fruit of the spirit. "But the fruit of the spirit is…patience"— (Galatians 5:22).

Being Long-Tempered

The word for patience in this verse is the Greek word, *Makrothumia.* It's actually two Greek words put together: *Makros*— meaning long, and *Thumos*—meaning temper. Literally it means long-tempered. The opposite would be short tempered, or short fused. So when a person has a short fuse or they lose their temper, they are not allowing the patience of Jesus to flow through their lives. We have all been there at times. You know what I mean. I lived in North Carolina for six years. We had moved to the south from New England, where we had lived for 22 years. One of the first things I discovered is that people in the south drive at a much slower pace than they do in the north. I would get steamed almost every time I stopped behind someone at a traffic light. It seems that green does not mean go. It means to start to think about going. I had one driver who sat so long, oblivious to the light, or the line of cars behind her, that the light turned yellow. At that point I had exhausted what little patience I had and blew the horn. I could see her jump as if startled into reality. But then she still sat there for a long time. She finally moved into the intersection when the light turned red. I was fuming, but none of the cars behind me ever honked their horns. It's as if everyone on the road was fine with it, except me. I know they are going to live much longer than me, because no one is stressed, pressured or in a hurry. I had many conversations with God while driving in the south.

Sometimes our impatience gets us into trouble. In 2006 Marcia and I built our dream house; a nice Cape Cod nestled in the woods. We had moved in over the weekend, and I had only a few more pieces of furniture to put in place. Marcia wanted me to get some help moving the love seat and couch from the basement into the living room. But I didn't want to wait. No one was home and I was determined to get everything done that afternoon. So I moved the couch around and L-shaped staircase from the basement to the living room all by myself.

It was a feat I was pretty proud of. Once I was at the top of the stairs, I was breathing so hard; I didn't want to lift any more weight. The couch was padded and fluffy, so I thought it would slide easily over the new hardwood floor. And it did—until I looked back and noticed there must have been a staple or something sticking out from the upholstery. Along the entire length of the new hardwood floor was a deep gouge. I don't think I have ever been so angry in my life. I sunk to my knees in the middle of the floor and yelled and cried and shouted a few choice words. It was a low moment, but my impatience got me there. So I know what it is to get impatient, and loose my cool.

Tipping the Scale From Anger To Sin

Impatience is when we are short-fused. It is when we get angry, but it's more than that. It's when we lose our temper. That takes anger to a different level. Impatience is when we tip the scale of anger in dip into sin. Getting angry and losing our temper are two different things. When we lose our temper we sin, but you can be angry without sinning. "Be angry, and yet do not sin"—(Ephesians 4:26a). That says you can be angry without sinning, but anger can lead to sin. The apostle goes on to describe how anger becomes sin. "Do not let the sun go down on your anger"—(Ephesians 4:26b). In other words, if we hold on to our anger it leads to a grudge. And that can lead to the devil having his way in our life. "And do not give the devil an opportunity"—(Ephesians 4:27).

Chuck Swindoll, in his book, *Anger,* lays out the different levels of anger. We can see from that, where sin enters into our hearts.

- Irritation—a feeling of discomfort brought about by someone or something.
- Indignation—a feeling that something must be answered; there must be a correcting of that which is wrong.

We can experience anger in that form without it falling into sin, but the next levels are problematic.

- Wrath—giving expression to a strong desire to avenge.
- Fury—the loss of emotional control.
- Rage—a temporary loss of control involving acts of violence. The angry person scarcely realizes what he has done.[50]

Impatience can do a lot of damage to relationships. "A hot-tempered person starts fights; a cool-tempered person stops them"—(Proverbs 15:18). "Sensible people control their temper; they earn respect by overlooking wrongs"—(Proverbs 19:11). Jesus fills us with His patience, but impatience blocks it from flowing through our lives. So the question is, how do we deal with impatience (a short fuse) so that the patience of Jesus can flow through our lives?

Solutions That Don't Work

Let me start by sharing two ways not to do it. First, we should not seek patience by praying for it—but not for the reason people may think. It's almost a cliché to hear people say, don't pray for patience or God will make your life really hard in order to develop it in you. God doesn't work that way. Actually the reason we don't pray for patience is because it doesn't work. God does not give patience like a gift. Patience is a result of something else. We will explore that idea in a minute.

The second way we should not seek patience is to take steps to deal with our anger. Anger management is not an effective strategy when dealing with impatience. I am not against anger management, but dealing with anger won't help when we have an impatience problem, because anger is a symptom of impatience, not a cause. If we are going to deal with our impatience, we must recognize the root causes of it, and then deal with those. I will share two common root causes for impatience. Those are the things we need to deal with in order to allow the patience of Jesus to flow through us. We have to remove the barriers so His Spirit can be expressed through our lives.

Root Causes

The first barrier is a lack of trust. God is in control of our lives and our schedules. "My future is in your hands"—(Psalm 31:15). "And we know that God causes everything to work together for the good of those who love God and are called according to his purpose for them"—(Romans 8:28). But the question is, do I really believe my times are in His hands? Do I really believe God is sovereign? Do I really believe God will get me where He wants me, when He wants me? My impatience betrays the fact that I don't really believe that. Therefore, my problem is a problem of trust. There are many in the Bible who had a difficult time trusting God and leapt ahead of Him.

God had promised Abram a son, but when he turned 75 he still had no children. He and his wife, Sarai, decided it was time to help God with His promise. Sarai suggested Abram sleep with her Egyptian maid, Hagar, who was young and able to bear children. Abram agreed—tough assignment, but take one for the team, right? Anyway, Ishmael was born, but he was not the child of promise. He became the child of problems. The conflict between Ishmael and Isaac, the promised son who was eventually born, only grew over time. Their descendants have been at war ever since and continue to this day. The Israeli-Palestinian conflict stems back to those two stepbrothers.

Job was patient but his wife was not. She got tired of his suffering and wanted him to rush things along! "His wife said to him, 'Are you still trying to maintain your integrity? Curse God and die'"—(Job 2:9). She just wanted him to get it over with. The comedian, Tim Hawkins, raises an interesting point about Job's wife. God allowed Satan to do anything he wanted to Job, except take his life. Job lost his children, his livestock, his buildings and his health. Everything was taken from him, except his wife. Hawkins quips that surely a demon must have mentioned it to Satan. "What about his wife", the demons asks. "Leave her alone", Satan answered, "I know what I'm doing."[51]

This comes down to trusting God and His timing. I hate it when we have to travel through Logan airport. It seems we always run into weather and delays. When our kids were young we landed there with little time to spare before our next flight. Of course, the connecting flight was in a different terminal and at the other extreme end of the airport. This was before the day when carry-on luggage was equipped with handles and wheels. The kids were too young to run through the airport, so I grabbed a child up in each arm and my wife, Marcia, grabbed the suitcases. We ran through the airport with arms loaded. By the time we got to the other end of the airport, we were soaked with sweat and exhausted. We didn't want to miss our connection because it was the last flight of the day going to Maine, our destination. The last thing we wanted was to have to stay the night in Boston and catch an early flight the next morning. What would we do with a six month old and an 18 month old in an airport overnight? So we beat it as fast as we could. When we got to our gate we were late, but relieved to discover our outgoing flight was delayed as well. We made our connection. I saw a life-principle in that experience. If God wants us on the next flight, He'll delay the plane. In other words, if we are responsible, and we still find the timing of our lives to be different than what we would like, it becomes an issue of trusting God with the timing.

Another root cause of impatience is a desire for control. We want others to conform to our expectations. In a May 2012 article, Natasha Crain tells the following story. "Two weeks ago, I received a notice from the Department of Motor Vehicles (DMV) that it was time to come in and renew my driver's license. I don't know what the DMV is like in other parts of the country, but in Southern California it is widely known to be a disaster – one that you don't set foot in without an appointment. I promptly made my appointment online and headed for the DMV one morning last week. As expected, the walk-in line was out the door. Never mind those people, I thought to myself. I brushed by them with my best "I have an appointment" demeanor, clutching my confirmation in hand, only to see a marginally shorter line ahead labeled "Appointments Wait Here." My sigh was loud enough to be heard in a 15-20 person radius. The line moved fairly quickly, but when there was only one person left ahead of me, it stopped moving. For some reason, this person's transaction was taking almost 20 minutes. I stared at the back of his tattooed head, evaluating his low hanging shorts and the big gold jewelry draped around his neck. Why can't this guy get his life together? Why can't he get his paperwork right? Why does this have to impact ME right now? I broke. I marched up to the counter next to him and asked the worker if there was someone else who could help me because this appointment was taking a "ridiculous amount of time." He shook his head and sent me back to wait. Two minutes later, the person ahead of me was done. I felt a knot in my stomach as he turned around, not knowing what to expect after I had been so rude. He nodded at me meekly and said kindly, "Thank you so much for your patience." Then he walked out the door. I felt two inches – no, one inch – tall. Had I been him, I would have offered the impatient person behind me a few rude comments in return. Instead, the person I had judged to be somehow less important or worthy than myself responded with kindness and Christ-like humility. Fast forward 10 minutes. I had to stand in line again, this time to have my picture taken. As if I hadn't just experienced the sobering kindness of the gang member, I was already anxiously shifting back and forth evaluating the group of three teenage boys in front of me. They were loud and obnoxious and somehow I had concluded they didn't deserve to have their pictures taken first. Then one turned to me with a big smile. "Hey, why don't you go ahead of us? There are three of us and only one of you, so it's no problem for you to go first!" I felt God throwing cold water on my face at that moment, trying to wake me up from my coma of arrogance. Twice in the span of an hour, strangers had exhibited humble and kind behavior that I lacked. I don't know if any of them were Christians, but they acted as Christians and I did not."[52]

When we are impatient with other people, we are saying we are more important than they are; that our needs are more important than their needs. We may not admit it, but deep inside, we want to manipulate them to get in line with our needs and schedule. That is completely contrary to how Paul teaches us to approach our relationships. "With humility of mind regard one another as more important than yourselves; do not merely look out for your own personal interests, but also for the interests of others"—(Philippians 2:3b-4).

When getting irritated because someone or something is holding us up, ask some questions: What am I really irritated about?

Am I being realistic? Am I being flexible? Do I think my life is more important than theirs? Am I letting go of control? Whose control am I fighting—theirs or God's? Can I really do anything to change this situation, and if not, why stress? Have I prayed about this and entrusted the situation to God?

People who want to control others miss the magic of the moment. Jesus visited the home of his friend, Lazarus and his two sisters, Martha and Mary. While Jesus was teaching in the main gathering room, Martha was busy, getting things ready for a meal. She was annoyed, because her sister, Mary, wasn't helping. Instead, she was sitting with the disciples listening to Jesus. The more Martha worked, the more annoyed she because about her sister. Mary got to sit in the room with Jesus and visit with Him, while she had to slave in the kitchen. The least Mary could do was help. Was Martha expected to wait on everyone? Finally, she couldn't take it anymore. She stomped into the gathering, interrupted Jesus and complained about her sister's lack of help. She wanted Jesus to dismiss Mary and make her help Martha with the meal. But Jesus wouldn't do it. He corrected Martha's wrong thinking. She wanted to control her sister and make her join Martha in the kitchen. In essence Jesus said to Martha, There is only one thing necessary. Mary chose to live in the moment. Martha was scattered and bothered about the environment around her, when the King of kings was teaching in her living room. The highest priority was to stop the busy work and listen to the Master. The meal could wait. This was a once in a lifetime moment. Martha needed to seize the moment as her sister Mary had done. That's what we have to learn to do, live in the moment. Richard Rohr calls it "the naked now."[53] The situation is raw with promise and we have but this moment to strip away the clutter that masks the potential magic and seize the opportunity.

The Potential For Magic

If we live in a pattern of missing the moment for the sake of lesser things, we need to repent. Patience calls us to surrender control of our lives to God and submit to His timing, sovereignty and providence. Every moment contains the potential for magic, if we will but rest long enough to see it. Our business blinds us to the opportunity to capture the "necessary thing." Another way of saying it is we need to learn to be still. "Be still and know that I am God"—(Psalm 46:10). "Be still in the presence of the LORD, and wait patiently for him to act"—(Psalm 37:7). "But they that wait upon the LORD shall renew their strength; they shall mount up with wings as eagles; they shall run, and not be weary; and they shall walk, and not faint—(Isaiah 40:31).

Not much is known about the hymn, *Be Still, My Soul*, or it author, Katherine von Schlegel. But the words are a great reminder that God is in control and we can be still, trusting in His sovereignty and providence.

1 Be still, my soul: the Lord is on thy side.
Bear patiently the cross of grief or pain.
Leave to thy God to order and provide,
who through all changes faithful will remain.
Be still, my soul: thy best, thy heavenly Friend
through thorny ways leads to a joyful end.

2 Be still, my soul: thy God doth undertake
to guide the future surely as the past.
Thy hope, thy confidence let nothing shake;
all now mysterious shall be bright at last.
Be still, my soul: the waves and winds still know
his voice who ruled them while he dwelt below.

3 Be still, my soul: the hour is hastening on
when we shall be forever with the Lord;
when disappointment, grief, and fear are gone,
sorrow forgot, love's purest joys restored.

Be still, my soul: when change and tears are past
all safe and blessed we shall meet at last.[54]

8

Learning To Look Around

There has always been a lot of controversy about Jesus, but one thing everyone agrees on—whether they are His friends or enemies, whether they believe He is God, or just a man—is that Jesus was kind. He was in fact the kindest person who ever lived. The principles of kindness Jesus taught were revolutionary. They are commonplace in our day, but they were original with Jesus and turned the culture upside down.

"If you are sued in court and your shirt is taken from you, give your coat, too. If a soldier demands that you carry his gear for a mile, carry it two miles. Give to those who ask, and don't turn away from those who want to borrow"—(Matthew 5:40-42). The Romans occupied Israel during Jesus' lifetime on earth. A solder was allowed to conscript a civilian to help carry a load up to one mile when needed. Jesus taught to literally go the extra mile, not because you have to, but because you are kind.

Jesus Taught About Kindness

Jesus illustrated what kindness looks like in the parable of the Good Samaritan. It was a story about a man who was travelling from Jerusalem and was mugged along the road and left for dead. Two religious Jews saw the man and crossed to the other side of the road and kept walking. The third passer-by was a Samaritan. "Going over to him, the Samaritan soothed his wounds with olive oil and wine and bandaged them"—(Luke 10:34-35). He saw a person in need, stopped what he was doing, and got involved and cared for him in a practical way. Then he put the man on his own donkey and took him to an inn. He thought beyond the immediate need to extended care, despite the inconvenience of having to walk out of his way to an inn where he took care of the injured man. He stayed over night and tended to the stranger's needs. "The next day he handed the innkeeper two silver coins, telling him, 'Take care of this man'"—(v.35). He gave the innkeeper money to care for the man because he didn't want to leave a burden with the innkeeper. "If his bill runs higher than this, I'll pay you the next time I'm here"—(v.35). He committed to follow up to make sure the man was completely cared for. He took responsibility even though this was not his concern. He made it his concern. He had the ability to perceive what was going on and knew what needed to be done. He got involved at personal expense and inconvenience.

Jesus Lived It

And what was remarkable about Jesus—and unlike the other religious leaders of His day—was that He lived out what He taught. For example, "The apostles returned to Jesus from their ministry tour and told him all they had done and taught. Then Jesus said, 'Let's go off by ourselves to a quiet place and rest awhile.' He said this because there were so many people coming and going that Jesus and his apostles didn't even have time to eat. So they left by boat for a quiet place, where they could be alone. But many people recognized them and saw them leaving, and people from many towns ran ahead along the shore and got there ahead of them. Jesus saw the huge crowd as he stepped from the boat, and he had compassion on them because they were like sheep without a shepherd. So he began teaching them many things"—(Mark 6:30-34). Jesus and His disciples were exhausted. They literally didn't have time to eat. They needed rest. But the people didn't care about that. They raced around the lake to meet Him. But instead of being frustrated, Jesus stepped up and helped them.

Of course the ultimate expression of kindness was Jesus' incarnation. He stooped down from the glory of heaven to become one of us. It was an act of humiliation beyond comprehension. And then to do so knowing He would be rejected by us and eventually crucified, was unrivaled kindness.

Live It Out

As followers of Christ we are expected to be kind. "Since God chose you to be the holy people he loves, you must clothe yourselves with tenderhearted mercy, kindness, humility, gentleness, and patience"—(Colossians 3:12). Paul described this as clothing ourselves. That speaks of a lifestyle, not just an occasional act. "In everything we do, we show that we are true ministers of God. We patiently endure troubles and hardships and calamities of every kind. We have been beaten, been put in prison, faced angry mobs, worked to exhaustion, endured sleepless nights, and gone without food. We prove ourselves by our purity, our understanding, our patience, our kindness, by the Holy Spirit within us, and by our sincere love"—(2 Corinthians 6:4-6). Here the Bible speaks of kindness in spite of difficulties. That's only possible because of the Holy Spirit within. This type of kindness is a fruit of the Spirit (Galatians 5:22).

But what does kindness mean? The word is an Anglo-Saxon word. It comes from the word kind or kin, which meant family. We use that same word today when we speak of family. We talk of someone being kin, or we speak of having a close kinship, or we use the word kindred. The word kin can also mean child. That's where we get the word kindergarten. So kindness came to mean gentle and caring affection toward a child, or a family member. The Greek word for "kindness" is *chrēstotēs*. It means tender concern. When you put that all together kindness means doing thoughtful deeds for others. But it's more than just doing something nice once in a while. It is the inclination of a person's character. When the Spirit works in us we begin doing kind deeds because we are kind. But the question is—are we kind?

Does the World Think of Kindness When
They Look at Christians?

In the early days of the church, followers of Jesus were known as Christos: Christians (Christ followers). Another way of saying it would be, "the Christ ones."[55] But the Greek word *Christos* is very similar to another Greek word, *Chrestos*. The word *Chrestos* means kind ones. One word is spelled with an "I" –*Christos*; the other with an "E" –*Chrestos*. Many people in the early years of the church confused the two. Instead of calling Jesus' followers *Christos*: Christians, they called them *Chrestos*: the kind ones. That seems fitting. They were not just known as the Christ-ones, but the kind-ones. The question is, would Christians today be identified by society as "the kind-ones"? I would say *yes*, on our good days, but sometimes not so much.

We are called to be kind. Jesus is kind and He is in us. But as with love, joy, peace and patience, there are things that block that fruit of His Spirit from flowing through our lives. So what is it that blocks us from being kind? We think the opposite of kindness is being mean, and in a sense that is right. But kindness—as illustrated in the Good Samaritan and in the Sermon on the Mount—is more about being aware of a need and helping others out. The opposite of kindness is apathy or indifference: being blinded to, or unaware of the needs around us, or not caring enough to get involved. So we have to deal with those if we want to remove the barriers so that the kindness of Jesus can flow through our lives. The way we remove the barrier is to identify the cause of apathy.

The Cause of Apathy

Sometimes we think people are apathetic and uncaring because they are selfish. Sometimes that may be true, but I think more often is it something else. I think a far more common reason people are apathetic is because they have lost hope. They are not selfish in the sense of being greedy, but they are self-focused in the sense of being defeated. As a result, they stop caring, which causes their eyes to shut to the needs of those around them. They can't see the needs of others around them, because they have no hope for themselves. They have given up on their goals. They stopped reaching for the call of God for their life, and thus became indifferent. People lose hope when they feel like it's too late to reach their goals; when they think God will no longer use them; when the passion of their heart cools. Their sense of call, purpose, significance and mission fades. In that state they are incapable of seeing the needs of others, let alone helping them. So if someone is going to be kind, they have to care. And if they are going to be healthy enough to care, they have to have hope. So the real question becomes, how do we gain hope?

How Do We Gain Hope?

The great thing about hope is that it is the inheritance of a child of God. Look at Romans 15:13. "Now may the God of hope fill you with all joy and peace in believing, so that you will abound in hope by the power of the Holy Spirit." Notice Paul called Him the God of hope. If you know the book of Romans, you know Paul could have called God any number of things—the God of grace, the God of power, the God of good news. But the label he chose was the God of hope.

The word Hope means expectation and anticipation. So we could say God is called the God of expectation. He is a God who is best characterized by expectation, anticipation, or hope. If we share life with Him, and He is the God of hope, then we should be the people of hope. That's how He expects us to operate. God never encourages His people to give up hope. It's just the opposite.

During the days of Elisha, king Joram and king Jehoshaphat joined forces and were marching against the king of Moab. They journeyed a seven day route through the desert to attack Moab. On the way, they ran out of water and there was none available. The prophet Elisha was summoned to seek counsel from the Lord. God told them to fill the valley full of ditches and they would miraculously fill with water. They had two armies and all their animals to water, so it would take a lot of water. They could have dug one large ditch, but God said to literally fill the valley full of ditches. As many ditches as they dug, that's how much water they would have. It was a picture of hope. If your hope is small, only dig three ditches, but if you believe, dig as many as you can and God will fill them. The amount of ditches was a measure of their amount of hope. And God did not want just a few, but He expected them to literally fill the valley with ditches.

God is disappointed when our hopes are too small. He expects us to believe Him to do great things. Another incident from the end of

Elisha's life reveals the level of hope God wants us to share. "When Elisha was in his last illness, King Jehoash of Israel visited him and wept over him. 'My father! My father! I see the chariots and charioteers of Israel!' he cried. Elisha told him, 'Get a bow and some arrows.' And the king did as he was told. Elisha told him, 'Put your hand on the bow,' and Elisha laid his own hands on the king's hands. Then he commanded, 'Open that eastern window,' and he opened it. Then he said, 'Shoot!' So he shot an arrow. Elisha proclaimed, 'This is the Lord's arrow, an arrow of victory over Aram, for you will completely conquer the Arameans at Aphek.' Then he said, 'Now pick up the other arrows and strike them against the ground.' So the king picked them up and struck the ground three times. But the man of God was angry with him. 'You should have struck the ground five or six times!' he exclaimed. 'Then you would have beaten Aram until it was entirely destroyed. Now you will be victorious only three times'" (2 Kings 13:14-19). It would please God for us to live in hope, since that is His nature. That means, as a Christian hope is our birthright. In other words, we are in relationship with the God who lives in the atmosphere of hope. Hope is to God what water is to a fish. He just lives in it. He is The God of hope.

A Prayer For Hope—Sort Of

But it's not automatic. That's why Paul actually prayed for us to have hope. Paul starts this verse with the word may—"**may** the God of hope fill you" (emphasis added). That indicates this is a prayer. Paul wanted God to do something in our lives. He wanted God to fill us, but notice Paul didn't pray we be filled with hope. Instead, he prayed we be filled with joy and peace—"may the God of hope fill you with all joy and peace." Why didn't he pray that God fill us with hope? I believe it is because hope is not something that is directly given, but instead, is the result of something else. If God gave hope directly, then Paul would have prayed the God of hope fill us with hope. But he didn't pray that. Hope is a gift from the God of hope, but He gives that hope indirectly by filling us with joy and peace.

Joy is an inner contentment with life that is based on the knowledge that our future is secure in the Presence of God. The peace of God is a protective armor around our heart and mind. There are so many outside influences that try to attack our hearts. The external pressures of life, trials and tragedies, hurtful people, the kingdom of darkness—all these things assault us and try to mess with our minds and harden our hearts, but God's peace is a barrier, a protection from those attacks. When we have joy—an inner contentment—and that joy is guarded by peace, it makes room for hope to thrive in our hearts.

A Gift From God, But We Have Our Part As Well

While it is true God makes it possible for hope to thrive in our hearts, there is something we have to do. Paul said the way God fills us with joy and peace, is in response to our believing—"Now may the God of hope fill you with all joy and all peace in believing." This is an important key to experiencing hope. Everything in this verse is done by God, except for this one thing, believing. That's our part, and it's the starting point for hope. The way the sentence is structured we can see the chain of events is very specific. We believe. Then God responds by filling us with joy and peace, and that leads to abounding in hope.

But notice something else as well. The word "believing" is general in nature. Paul didn't tell us anything specifically in which to believe. We are simply instructed to believe. The word is also in the present tense; it's not believe, but believing. That means we are to be in a continuous state of believing. Let me share two similar statements. Grammatically they are pretty much the same, but theologically they are very different. Here's the first sentence: I believe in God. Here's the second: I believe God. Believing in God means you acknowledge who He is and you place your trust in Him for salvation. Believing God means you believe what He says; you believe His promises, His word. That's what Paul meant here by the word believing; that you believe what God says. And because it's in the present tense, it means he was describing the general practice of our lives. That wording is intentional. Paul was not speaking about believing a specific truth; he was talking about believing in general. Now here's why this is so amazing. Notice the word hope is also general in nature. Paul didn't say to hope in any specific thing; only that hope abounds in us. Instead of it being a specific hope, it's more of an atmosphere. See how Paul said it in the text, "abound in hope."

He wanted us to live in an atmosphere of hope. Why? Because to live in a hopeful state sets the environment so that when a specific hope is needed we already have the environment established so that something can happen. How can we build up any kind of specific hope, if we don't live in a hope-filled environment? We can't. So this is a general atmosphere of hope that gets us set so we are ready when we do need to focus on a specific thing. And that's why joy and peace are so important, because they are generalized as well.

Notice how Paul described them as *all* joy and *all* peace. That's not specific, that's wide ranging. Paul was dealing with fundamental, foundational things that we need to have in place in our hearts. A general sense of joy and peace is vital in order to create the atmosphere where we can live in a hopeful state. So a general course of believing begins to change the atmosphere. The temperature moves toward joy and peace, which in turn changes our environment to one of hopefulness. That gets us ready so when we do need to latch onto something specific, all the necessary attitudes are already in place. Believing God—believing His word—means trusting and obeying. As we walk in trust and obedience, the Holy Spirit responds by filling us with all joy and all peace, and that results in abundant hope.

Our Job Is To Believe

All we have to do is believe. Jesus said, "this is the work of God, that you believe"—(John 6:29). We believe in God, but do we believe God? And when we live in a hopeful atmosphere our eyes are now open to the calling of God; there is purpose, meaning and significance. When we live that way we are free to see the needs of others so we are no longer apathetic, and can allow the fruit of kindness to flow through our lives. But in all of this, belief is the key. We have to believe God to live life in an atmosphere of hope. Then we have to develop awareness of our surroundings and learn to listen and watch to see those in need. And then we are to act.

Belief in God can evidence nothing more than mere intellectual assent, but believing God affects everything. When we believe God, we are saying He is right about everything and it is of paramount importance for us to harmonize our lives with His reality.

Michael Patton expressed the idea this way. "Think of life like a car. Most people I know have God in one of four places in their car: 1. The trunk. In this sense, God is the "go-to" God when we are in trouble. Like with the spare tire, the tool kit, or the flashlight, we only call upon him when we are in desperate need. Other than that, he has no part to play in our daily living. We believe in him, but we don't believe him enough to let him out of the trunk. 2. The Back seat. This represents a heightened conviction about the need for God in our lives, but we don't really want him bothering us. He is like a back seat driver who is constantly whining about what direction we are going, telling us to turn here rather than there. We would like him to just be quite, but we are willing to put up with his disruptions in order to feel better about our conviction that we need him in our lives. 3. The passenger seat. This person is very convicted about their need for God so they allow him to be right beside them. In fact, this person likes God quite a bit. They enjoy the conversation and even ask for suggestions about where to turn and how fast to go. We are so proud about this level of involvement that we create bumper stickers to let others know that 'God is my co-pilot'. However, God is not calling us to any of these first three. I am not saying that if you find God in your passenger seat, back seat, or, even, trunk you are not a Christian. That is not the issue. I am talking about what it means to believe God. 4. The driver's seat. This is where God wants to be. This is where we graduate from believing in God to believing God. This is where we hand control of everything to him. This is where he is no longer just a god in our lives, but our God. He says to us, 'Give me the driver's seat of your life. I want nothing less. Believe me; I know much more than you do. I want control of your passions, your plans, your family, where you are going, and where you have been. My way is the best. I know you better than you know yourself. I know you believe in me, but will you believe me. You sit there in the passenger seat and I will take care of the rest. And please…no back seat driving.'"[56]

Think about some of these issues: If I believe God, do I pray about everything? If I believe God, do I trust He will work everything out for His glory? If I believe God, do I take His word over my own opinion? If I believe God, do I judge Him when things go wrong? When we live that way, it allows hope to spring up in us, but many have lived so long with their eyes turned inward, they have forgotten how to look around.

Learning To Look Around

Below I have included an exercise to help us begin to look around. When we intentionally practice random acts of kindness, looking for opportunities to be a blessing to others, it begins to train us to look around. You can find thousands of such lists on the Internet. I Googled random acts of kindness and scrolled through many pages of options. I randomly chose the list below.

1. Purchase coffee for a stranger
2. Write a letter or card to a friend
3. Donate toys to someone in need
4. Take some canned food to the pantry
5. Pick up the tab for a stranger
6. Clean up some litter at a local park
7. Leave a treat for the mailman
8. Make cookies for the neighbor
9. Take a treat to the police/fire department
10. Help someone carry grocery bags
11. Walk dogs at the dog shelter
12. Bring doughnuts (or a healthy treat, like cut-up fruit) to work.
13. While you're out, compliment a parent on how well-behaved their child is.
14. Cook a meal or do a load of laundry for a friend who just had a baby or is going through a difficult time.

15. If you walk by a car with an expired parking meter, put a quarter in it.
16. Each time you get a new piece of clothing, donate an old one.
17. Email or write an old teacher who made a difference in your life.
18. Compliment someone to their boss.
19. Leave a nice server the biggest tip you can afford.
20. Talk to the shy person who's sitting by themselves at a party.
21. Help a mother with her baby stroller.
22. Give someone a book you think they'd like.
23. Be the person who puts a tip in the tip jar at the coffeeshop. (Fewer people tip than you'd think!)
24. If you spill creamer or sugar on the counter at Starbucks, wipe it up.
25. Call your grandparents. Call them!
26. When you're throwing something away on the street, pick up any litter around you and put that in the trash too.
27. Write something nice on that person's updates who posts on Facebook constantly. They're probably lonely.
28. Send anonymous flowers to the receptionist at work.
29. Play board games with senior citizens at a nursing home. Sixty percent of them will never have a visitor during their stay.
30. Babysit for a single mom for free.
31. Adopt a rescue pet.
32. Leave some extra quarters in the laundry room.
33. Say thank you to a janitor.
34. Send dessert to another table.
35. Wash someone's car.
36. Keep an extra umbrella at work and let someone borrow it on their way home if there's a sudden downpour.
37. Make two lunches and give one away.
38. Say yes at the store when the cashier asks if you want to donate $1 to whichever cause.
39. Be kind to the customer service rep on the phone. It's not their fault.
40. Offer to return a shopping cart to the store for someone loading groceries in their car.[57]

Connecting The Dots

Let's wrap this all up by connecting the dots. Jesus wants to express the fruit of kindness through our lives. Apathy blocks kindness from flowing through us. Apathy comes from a lack of hope. Hope is restored when we learn to believe God, for believing God causes us to abound in joy and peace. Joy and peace create an atmosphere of hope, and hope will open the door to awareness of the needs of others so that kindness can be released.

9
The Spiritual Sweet Spot

I enjoy watching those restoration house shows. They take a dated home and transform it into a model home. Almost every show has the dramatic reveal. The couple walks in the front door. Their eyes are wide and their jaws drop and just as they get ready to speak, they break for a commercial. But when they return, the first words that almost always come out of one of their mouths is "Oh my God!" Have you noticed? That's what they say almost every time. It catches my attention because that would have never happened in my home. When I was a kid, we were not allowed to say something like that. That was considered taking God's name in vain. If I had said, "Oh my God!" I would have been eating a bar of soap. So instead, we said, "Oh my goodness!" It meant the same thing, but somehow it seemed more sanitized. Goodness was a substitute for God, which makes sense because we equate goodness with God. It's part of our culture. We grew up praying for meals, using the child's prayer—"God is great. God is good. Now we thank Him for our food." Often in church we would hear the worship leader say, "God is good" to which we were to respond, "All the time." And then he would reverse it. "All the time" and we would finish, "God is good."

We have equated good with God. But the word good has been watered down in our culture. We say things like, "Good job." "He was a good man." What a good dog!" How many times have we heard Lucy say, "Good grief, Charlie Brown!" We use the word in a variety of ways. Good has become relative. We each determine what is good for us. The world says good is everything from abstaining from war to saving the polar bears. But the world also says good is providing federal funding for abortion, or offering contraception for minors without parental consent. It is like the definitions for good and evil have been flipped around. We are living in the day Isaiah warned us about. "Woe to those who call evil good, and good evil; who substitute darkness for light and light for darkness; who substitute bitter for sweet and sweet for bitter—(Isaiah 5:20).

Goodness Lost

In the beginning all man knew was good. He walked each day in the garden with God. His life was spent in unbroken fellowship with God. But then the temptation came to eat from the tree of the knowledge of good and evil. Adam already knew good. He lived it everyday with the Lord. But now he would learn evil. But think about what that means. If we were able to live on the surface of the Sun, we would not have any concept of darkness. Every place we looked, there would be light. The only way we could understand darkness, is if we could descend into a cave. Have you ever been in a cave under the earth where there is total darkness? At one point, when visiting such a cave, the tour guide turned out the lights. We stood in the complete absence of light. I held my hand inches from my face, but could not see it. Total blackness. I thought I knew dark before, but I didn't really understand it until all light was completely removed. We can only know darkness by being removed from the light. We can only know evil by turning away from good—by turning away from God. The small print the serpent neglected to tell Adam was that the way he would know evil was by being separated from God. Sin made a separation between the primal couple and their God. It's not that God cast them out, but sin revealed how unlike God they were and out of fear they hid themselves from Him. God in His grace sought them out, but still there was a wedge that could only be healed by destroying the power of sin. Jesus' death on the cross and subsequent resurrection reconciled that separation. Jesus reintroduced mankind to God. He opened the door to once again experience good. Now goodness, which is an aspect of His character has come into our lives via the Holy Spirit. As Galatians 5:22-23 says, "The fruit of the Spirit is…goodness."

Calling Everything Back to Good

In the last chapter we saw that kindness involved doing nice deeds for people. Goodness and kindness are similar, but goodness goes further than kindness. Goodness not only involves doing kind things, but as Julie Powers put it, goodness means participating with

God in the kingdom work of calling everything back to good.[58] It's about bringing things back to God's purpose. Sometimes that means doing nice things for people, but sometimes it involves correction. Goodness is about doing whatever is necessary to align things with God's purpose.

Jesus is the ultimate example of goodness. He showed tender compassion, but at times He was tough. When He confronted Peter after His resurrection, He kindly reiterated His desire for Peter to serve in His Kingdom, but also directly and firmly confronted Peter's sin. Jesus didn't sweep it under the rug, but He also didn't allow it to stand in the way of His purposes. When Jesus challenged Nicodemus, He was kind, but firm. Nicodemus was a proud teacher of the Law and needed to be confronted at the point of his pride. John's gospel records the exchange between he and Jesus. "After dark one evening, he came to speak with Jesus. 'Rabbi,' he said, 'we all know that God has sent you to teach us. Your miraculous signs are evidence that God is with you.' Jesus replied, 'I tell you the truth, unless you are born again, you cannot see the Kingdom of God.' 'What do you mean?' exclaimed Nicodemus. 'How can an old man go back into his mother's womb and be born again?' Jesus replied, 'I assure you, no one can enter the Kingdom of God without being born of water and the Spirit. Humans can reproduce only human life, but the Holy Spirit gives birth to spiritual life. So don't be surprised when I say, "You must be born again." The wind blows wherever it wants. Just as you can hear the wind but can't tell where it comes from or where it is going, so you can't explain how people are born of the Spirit.' 'How are these things possible?' Nicodemus asked. Jesus replied, '**You are a respected Jewish teacher, and yet you don't understand these things**?'"— (John 3:2-10 emphasis added).

When Jesus defended His Father's honor, He made a whip and drove unscrupulous moneychangers from the Temple. He was angered they had turned a place of worship into a money laundering operation. He was bringing the Temple use back into alignment with the purposes of God. When He did this, the disciples remembered the prophecy that said zeal for God's house would consume the Messiah (John 2:17). Jesus was gentle with people, but violent with sin. His death dealt a crushing blow to the power of sin and the weapons of the devil (Romans 8:3; 1 John 3:8).

The fruit of goodness works in a couple of different ways. First, goodness desires to keep people on God's desired path. Paul hinted at this when he gave instruction to the Galatian church. "Dear brothers and sisters, if another believer is overcome by some sin, you who are godly should gently and humbly help that person back onto the right path"—(Galatians 6:1). Correction is not about embarrassing, punishing or condemning someone who has fallen. The goal is to set the person right again. Many years ago we had a leader in our church who had cheated on his wife. When his sin came to light I immediately met with him and our board of elders. We were not there to judge or belittle him. He was embarrassed and broken enough as it was. The Holy Spirit was heaping conviction on him. We didn't need to add to that. Our place was to come alongside he and his wife and help them put their marriage back together, if possible, and to help him heal spiritually. He stepped down from his leadership position so he could dedicate his full attention to reconciling with his wife. It took many months and many hours of discipleship and counseling, but in time they were reunited. I will never forget the leaders in that congregation. They didn't want to hurt the man. He was guilty and in the wrong, but they saw a brother who needed to be helped, not an enemy who needed to be attacked. In time he was restored to spiritual leadership within the fellowship. It doesn't always work out this way, but I am grateful that situation ended in a win. But if the leaders of the church had thought that goodness was only about punishing sin and demanding conformity to God's Law, then this story most likely would have turned out very differently. Instead, they saw their role, not as the morality police, but as rescuers seeking to save a family from destruction.

The Opposite of Goodness

We think of the opposite of goodness as evil. The Genesis story confirms that, but we best not isolate the concept of evil to satanic darkness. I believe we fight against good in more subtle ways; chief among them is neglect. For example, I had a friend who, years ago, was engaged to marry a woman who turned out to be unfaithful. During their engagement period, I observed her and had a thousand red flags screaming in my mind that this marriage was doomed. I loved my friend, but I didn't say anything. I didn't want to confront him. For one thing, I thought he would never listen to me, but the greater resistance was the fear of rejection. I did my friend a great disservice. Even if he had not listened to me, if I really loved him, I should have said something. I decided from then on not to let that happen again.

After being in the ministry for many years, I have learned that morality police are the exception, not the norm. Most people run away from confrontation—even when they shouldn't. People hate conflict and don't want to be seen as judgmental. Confrontation feels like we are standing over someone in condemnation and self-righteousness. A number of years ago the show American Idol had a woman on who was a horrible singer. Early on in the season they have the good, the bad and the ugly. She was bad. Unfortunately, no one in her life ever told her that. Each judge commented on her performance. They were trying to be honest, but kind. But then it was Simon Cowell's turn to critique her. He started by saying, "That was absolutely the most…" He paused. Her eyebrows raised in anticipation of everything her family probably ever said to her. But then he went on. "…the most awful performance I have ever heard." She sunk right there. You could see the devastation on her face. She was totally embarrassed. Evidently no one ever told her she was terrible. If she had delusions of a musical career, she definitely needed are reality check, but not like that. Not on national television. She was bad, but the at that moment, the bad guy seemed like Simon. He came to be the one we loved to hate, because he would be brutally blunt with people. That's the image I get in my mind when I think about confrontation. I don't want to be seen as a Simon Cowell.

But when Paul said we are to confront those who fall into sin, that's not the picture he had in mind. When we confront someone who is off the right path, we need to see it more like we are jumping into the ditch with them and saying, "Okay, I am here by your side. Let's lock arms and get out of this together." When Paul wrote in Galatians 6:1 to "help that person back onto the right path" he used a Greek word that had medical implications. It's a word that described setting a broken bone. I am told that when a bone heals from a break, it is stronger at the place of the break than what it was before the break. Paul was admonishing us to help our brothers and sisters reset their spiritually broken bones with the hopes they will come out stronger than before. Can you think of anyone you need to have an honest heart-to-heart with? Why not rebuke the fear, step out in faith and be an agent of God's goodness and love.

Finding Your Sweet Spot

Another way goodness is seen is that it wants to keep things aligned with God's intended purposes. After the first day of creation in the book of Genesis, God assessed His work and said it was good. At the end of each day He said the same things. Seven times the book records God Saying, "It was good" (Genesis 1:4, 10, 12, 18, 21, 25, 31). It all was good because each part of creation performed its expected function. When applied to us, goodness is about fulfilling our calling and purpose. God has a plan for each of us. We are "good" when living in that plan.

Some people are just existing, surviving, waiting for heaven. God has better things for us. In studio city Los Angeles is a beautiful 1961 red and white Corvette convertible. It's located at the studio city car wash, mounted 30 feet above the parking lot on a signpost. What a waste! That car has totally missed its purpose. It should be flying down the highway, entered into car shows, or sitting in my garage—just kidding, sort of. God doesn't want that to be your life: sitting on display as a spiritual trophy. He wants us to live to our full potential, to operate in what I call our spiritual sweet spot. That's what God considers good.

There are some signs that a person is living outside their spiritual sweet spot. A person who lives in a continual state of frustration may be living outside their sweet spot. It's like trying to force a square peg into a round hole; you're doing what's expected of you, but there is no fulfillment. It seems like you are just putting in the time to draw a paycheck, but you are frustrated, restless; feeling like there is so much more, but you are missing it.

Another sign is burnout. Elijah is a classic example of this. He faced the prophets of Baal in a showdown on Mount Carmel. He challenged the 450 prophets to a sort of duel. An altar was built and a sacrifice was placed on it. Each side was to pray to their god and the god who answered by fire would show himself to be the true god. The Baal worshippers went first. They prayed, cried, shouted, danced, cut themselves—anything they could do to get their god to respond. But in their heaven, there was nothing but crickets. Elijah mocked them, suggesting perhaps their god was on vacation or taking a nap. Finally, once all their energy and blood was drained, Elijah took his turn. But he offered a few changes before he prayed. He had a trench dug around the altar and had water poured on the altar—so much water that it filled the trench. If fire came, no one could say it was some kind of trick. When Elijah prayed to God, fire fell from heaven—enough fire to burn up the sacrifice, disintegrate the rocks and drink up all the water in the trench. It was frighteningly clear; Jehovah was the true God. Elijah then turned on the prophets of Baal and had the people cut them down with the sword. It was a high moment in Elijah's life. But when Queen Jezebel caught word of what happened, she was enraged. She was a follower of Baal and hated Elijah's God. She threatened to kill the prophet. One moment Elijah is the brave hero, championing the causes of God, and the next moment his is running to hide in fear. He spent several days in the wilderness, alone and feeling defeated. Even though the prophets of Baal had been defeated, Baalism hadn't. The queen would make sure it continued in the land. He felt alone. He wanted to quit. He wanted to die. He begged God to take his life. At one point he complained to God that he was all alone in this quest to rid Israel of the false religion. Something snapped and he didn't care anymore. He just wanted out. Burnout sneaks up on you. You are pushing and pushing, and them something suddenly changes inside. You feel alone, defeated, sorry for yourself. You want to quit, and even despair of life. Those are common symptoms of someone pushing hard outside their sweet spot.

When someone lives or works outside their sweet spot they can exert a lot of effort for very little fruit. They work harder, but get less done. I remember when I was a kid and got my first ten speed bike. That was freedom. It is to a ten year old what getting your first car is to a teenager. I had to get used to shifting the gears at first. On one occasion I had been cruising along in tenth gear and had to stop. I was at the base of a hill and when the traffic was clear I took off, but I was still in top gear. Riding up a hill in tenth gear from a dead stop is not productive. You strain and push as hard as you can, but you don't get very far. When you work outside your sweet spot, that's what it's like. How different it is when serving in your wheelhouse. There is accelerated achievement. There is still work to do, but the greater the effort the greater the result.

Another sign someone is outside his or her sweet spot is mission drift. They find themselves moving away from the passions that originally fueled their heart. Harvard University originally only employed Christian professors. Their stated mission was to instruct students to "know God and Jesus Christ." But they had long since moved away from that original passion.

Howard Pew and his family were strong Christians. The Pew family made a lot of money in the oil business. When they desired to be generous with their wealth, they set up a foundation that ultimately became the Pew Charitable Trusts. Howard Pew wanted all donations to only be made to organizations that were faithful to the Gospel; ministries like the Billy Graham evangelistic association. But after the founder died, this charitable foundation drifted significantly, funding organizations that Howard Pew and his family would never have approved, such as Planned Parenthood and many Ivy League schools.

George Williams first started the Young Man's Christian Association (YMCA) as a Bible study for displaced men in London, England. The core of this group was centered on learning about Christ, eventually training and commissioning over 20,000 missionaries. But as the organization grew and expanded to other countries, the focus became all about health and fitness with no reference to Christ. In 2010, the organization officially dropped three of its four letters to become simply The Y, removing any remaining ties to its Christian roots.[59]

Another sign we are working outside our spiritual sweet spot, is having no time for key relationships. We are like Jesus' friend, Martha. We are always in a rush to get things done, focusing more on the immediate tasks at hand, rather than the people in our lives. Mary, her sister, was content to let the chores set for a moment while she sat at Jesus' feet to hear Him teach. She knew it was a rare opportunity to have the Master in her home and she wanted to take advantage of it. Martha couldn't stop to be with the Lord or the friends who had gathered in her living room. She had to make sure everything was perfect for the visit. What made it perfect was that Jesus was there, and He didn't come to see her house. He came to see her. Martha allowed unnecessary pressures to squeeze out time for important connection with family and friends. We can do the same if we are running outside our sweet spot.

Some Things to Think About

So how do we live out the fruit of goodness? How do we live in our spiritual sweet spot? Brad Lomenick asks six questions to help us discern what our life should be. What are your passions and gifts? There are things we are really good at and there are things we love to do. At the intersection of these two elements, we will find our life's purpose. Second, what would you work on or want to do for free? The answer to that question is usually a good sign of what God has designed you to do. Third, what energized you when you were a child? Does it still motivate you now? Knowing your calling is often directly connected to a childhood passion. When I was about four years old I remember my parents asking me to tell someone at church what I wanted to be when I grew up. Most kids answer something along the lines of a policeman, fireman, rock singer, movie star, etc. My answer was different. I said I wanted to be a preacher with gray hair. That was a driving passion, even at four. Though I strayed from the path for a season of my life, that call never left me. I began preaching at 21 and my hair was graying at 30. Don't dismiss those childhood dreams. They may be a key to your sweet spot. Fourth, if you could do anything and not fail, what would that be? The next questions are really coaching questions and deserve some serious consideration. If you are using this guide for discipleship, may I suggest you talk through these with your discipler? What barriers are preventing you from pursuing your true calling? Can you begin removing those? If you aren't engaging your gifts and talents where you find yourself now, could you make changes in your current role to better engage those? [60]

As you work through those questions it would be helpful to write down some smart goals that may come out of your conversation. Remember, a smart goal has to be specific, measurable, achievable, realistic and time-stamped.

10
The Glass Door

King David and his men were riding out of Jerusalem, perhaps for the last time. It was one of the darkest days of his life. His kingdom had been over thrown and he was escaping. While leaving the city a man named Shimei, a relative of Saul, David's predecessor, ran alongside David and his men. He was mocking and cursing David, throwing stones at him. He said David was a man of bloodshed and was getting what he deserved. This was God's curse on him and Shimei hoped David would rot. One of David's servants turned to David and said, "This insolent dog doesn't deserve to live. Let me go over and take off his head." But David stopped him and said "there will be no more bloodshed today. Maybe his curses are true. Perhaps God is bring on my head the things I deserve."

It had all started about 11 years earlier. David had many different wives, many of them political alliances. So David had many children who were half brothers and sisters with each other. One of David's sons, Amnon, burned with lust for Tamar, his half-sister. His cousin, who was a shrewd man, said he had a plan that would get Amnon what he wanted. He told Amnon to pretend he was sick and when his father, David, asked about him, he was to say the one thing that would make him feel better is if his sister Tamar would bake him some cakes and bring them to him in his apartment. David agreed and told Tamar to do as Amnon wished. When she arrived he asked her to serve them to him in his bed, and then ordered the house servants to leave. While feeding him the cakes, he raped her. When begging him not to do it, she offered to marry him first, saying it would save her reputation and his also. But he ignored her. When he was done, he ordered her out, for the disgust he felt for her after rapping her was greater than the lust he felt beforehand. She again begged him to marry her for to violate her virginity and then kick her to the curb would destroy any chance of her having a future husband. But he was ruthless and uncaring.

Tamar ran away, devastated and destroyed. Her full brother, Absalom saw her and figured out what had happened. He had her move into his home and told her to keep quite about it. David was angry when he heard what had happened, but he didn't do anything to Amnon. He just wanted to pretend nothing happened. Absalom was not so forgiving, but he was cunning. He treated Amnon like he had always done, not raising any suspicion about how he really felt. He hated Amnon and was angered at his father for doing nothing. After two years, when the incident had been forgotten by most, he hosted a dinner with all his half-brothers. It was away from the city, to celebrate the harvest. During the party his assassins killed Amnon. The other brothers fled in the chaos, but it was known who orchestrated the murder. Absalom ran away to his grandfather's home. He was a king of another city state, for this had been one of David's political marriages. He hid out there for three years.

Finally, after David's anger had cooled he allowed Absalom to return to Jerusalem, but he was not allowed at court. He was mostly confined to his quarters. Absalom wanted to speak with his father. Yes, he had murdered his half-brother, but justice needed to be done and David wasn't going to do anything to make things right. David refused to see Absalom. It seemed as if David was more angry that Absalom had carried out justice than he was that Amnon had raped Tamar. Every time Absalom sent a request to see the king, it was ignored. He even tried to get to Joab, David's general. But Joab would not respond to his requests. So Absalom had his servants burn Joab's fields down. That got his attention. Absalom said it was the only way he could get someone's attention to be able to see the king.

David consented. The two met briefly, but nothing came of it. He was once again banished from David's presence. Absalom was so enraged he set out on a campaign to overthrow his father's thrown. Everyday he would sit at the city gates and meet the people who came to see David for a court ruling. When he would greet a person, they would bow, but he would quickly raise them to their feet so they felt like he was treating them like an equal. Then he would promise that if he were in charge he would have ruled on their case in a way that was favorable to them. Over a three year period he won the hearts of the people. That's when he raised an army to overthrow his father's throne.

That's why David was fleeing Jerusalem. He was heart broken that his son would seek to kill him and he was carrying the guilt for his pathetic parenting. David had planted a spy in the city and his men out fought Absalom, and so in time Absalom was killed and David was back in power. He and his men were returning to Jerusalem, bruised, but triumphant. Once again, he was in power with no rivals to challenge his throne. When he came to the Jordan River to cross back into his kingdom, there were a thousand people waiting on the other shore to welcome him home. And at the front of the crowd was Shimei, the little rat who was cursing David when he was fleeing. Shimei threw himself at David's feet, apologizing for his insolence, pledging his fidelity and praising the greatness of David's reign. It was all a sham. He was only interested in saving his own neck. David saw through the hypocrisy and so did his men. Again, one of David's men asked to chop off Shimei's head. David's position when crossing the river was now very different than it was before. Now David was in power. Now David had control with no one to challenge him. This little gnat who was kneeling before David did not deserve to live and David had every right and all the power to end his miserable life. But instead, David said no. There had been enough bloodshed. It was time for it to stop.

He had all the power and authority, but he chose to hold back. That is a picture of gentleness. In Galatians where it says the fruit of the Spirit is gentleness, the word that is used in the Greek is a word that was used to describe the controlling of a horse. Horses are bigger, stronger, faster and heavier then people. A horse could easily kill a man, but with a small bit and bridle, a man can guide a horse to walk, trot, canter, gallop, turn, go backwards and stop. When a person is sitting on a horse, they are sitting on raw power. Yet with the reigns, they are controlling the horse. That was the picture used to capture the word gentleness. It is power under control.

Gentleness Is Not Weakness

We mistakenly equate gentleness with weakness. But it is just the opposite. It's a thrill for a new father to hold the hand of his baby. The little fingers are so small they can only wrap around his thumb. If the baby squeezed as hard as he could the father would think it was cute. On the other hand, if the father chose to squeeze the baby's hand as hard as he could, he would crush the baby's hand. The baby can't be gentle because it has no power. Only the father who has power can choose to hold back and be gentle. The child who is weak cannot be gentle. Only the strong can be gentle.

The opposite of gentleness is not assertiveness or power. Jesus was gentle, yet He had the power to command nature. When He was asleep in the bow of the fishing boat on the Sea of Galilee, the disciples awakened Him because of a threatening storm. He spoke one simple statement, "Peace be still," and instantly the wind stopped blowing and the sea was as calm as glass. The disciples wondered who this man was that He could command the wind and waves. They were suddenly more terrified of Him than they were the storm. Jesus was gentle, but he possessed ultimate power. That's because only the powerful can be gentle. The opposite of gentleness is not power, but it is the abuse of power, which actually demonstrates true weakness.

The Abuse of Power

When Rehoboam took over the throne from his father Solomon, his advisors suggested he lower taxes. Solomon had levied a burden on the people and this would be a way of incurring favor with them. But Rehoboam's younger friends, who had not served in government, but were his new counselors advised the opposite. They said that if he lowered taxes he would be seen as weak. He took their advice and told the people that if his father Solomon had bound them with chains, he would bind them with scorpions. His insecurity led him to abuse his new found power and it revealed his real weakness. It also fractured the kingdom. The incident led to a civil split from which the nation never recovered.

Someone said at one time that absolute power corrupts absolutely. That is perhaps no more true than in the case of North Korea's leader, Kim Jong-Un. He is worshipped as a god and believes his own press. During a staff meeting this last year, one of his education ministers, Ri Yong-jin fell asleep. Jong-Un was so angered, he brought disciplinary actions against the minister. But he didn't dock his pay, or fire him from his job, or even send him to jail. No. Instead he had him shot, and not by any ordinary firing squad. He was shot with an anti-aircraft machine gun[61]. The upside is no one will ever fall asleep in another staff meeting.

We can see the abuse of power and real power contrasted with Jesus and His disciples. They were heading back to Jerusalem from the north, when they came to a Samaritan city. The people of the city met them at the boarder and refused them passage, insisting they walk around. The Samaritan town folk didn't want any Jews walking through their village. The disciples were incensed. How dare these Samaritan treat them that way! They turned to Jesus and insisted He call down fire from heaven and destroy the city like Sodom and Gomorrah. They had no power, but wanted Jesus to use His to answer their insult. Jesus had ultimate power, but chose to extend mercy. That's gentleness.

Why do we abuse power? We all do it to some extent or another. Maybe it's insecurity or fear, like the bully on the playground. That's probably a good deal of what is going on with Kim Jong-Un, though he is also crazy. I suspect the more common reason is that we value position more than life. That may sound strange at first, but let me show you what I mean. Let's say you are walking in the woods and you come across a bear. No matter how experienced you are in the woods, that's going to get your attention. You will show that bear respect because he can eat you. On the other hand, if you were walking in those same woods and stepped on a rock and in doing so, crushed an ant, it wouldn't even register. It would be a non-event. You respect the bear more than the ant because the bear is higher on the food chain. The ant feels pain just like the bear. The ant had a drive to survive and is as much alive as the bear. But the bear has a higher position than the ant. You may think, *this is stupid, you're talking about animals and ants*. But we do this with people too. Who do you show more respect for when entering a bank, the CEO or the janitor? Do you show more respect toward the school superintendent or the bus driver? They all possess life and are equally important to God, but we tend to show deference toward one more than the other because one is higher on the corporate food chain.

We may not be like Kim Jong-Un, but what about the times when we have the power to tell someone off, or be mean to them? Do we choose to attack, or refrain? The use of power is vital to relationships. Imagine a glass door standing between you and your goal. That glass door represents another person, a relationship. You can go through that door with grace to get to your goal, or you can shatter the glass door. There are all kinds of behaviors that shatter the glass door of a relationship; outbursts of anger, selfishness, pride, careless words, etc. We can get to where we want to go, but we trample on someone's feelings in the process, or we hurt someone, or betray them to get what we want. Those kinds of behaviors shatter the glass door of relationships. How can we move toward our goals without shattering the door? Gentleness is the key to moving toward our goals without hurting relationships. When dealing with people, there are three ways to approach them that will help us to keep the glass door of a relationship in tact.

Three Keys to Gentleness

1. Tempo. This refers the speed, pace or meter. A fast song has a fast tempo. A slow song has a slow tempo. The Bible speaks about the tempo we should assume when dealing with people. "You must all be quick to listen, slow to speak, and slow to get angry"— (James 1:19). These are connected like dominoes. The only way to be quick to listen is if we are slow to speak. In theory that ought to be easy, but in practice it's a different story. How many times when we are talking with people do we really listen to what they are saying? Are we watching their body language? Are we seeking to empathize and enter into their perspective? Or are we thinking about our response? If we are quick to speak, we can't be quick to hear. One cancels out the other. And if we don't truly listen, but instead are eager to share our perspective or opinion, then it will quickly escalate to anger. A sage once said if you want to find the truth, get rid of your opinions. I can hardly watch the news anymore because they place people of opposing

views on a panel and then let them talk over one another. It's a cacophony of noise and no one is listening to the other. I literally hate it. But aren't I engaging in some lesser version of that when I don't listen to the person who is talking to me? And if it hinders a relationship, then it's really not a lesser version, but actually a more serious offense. Glass door shattered. But if we stop to listen and talk to honestly try and understand the other person, we will get closer to a place or resolution. Perhaps we can move through the door without destroying it.

2. Tone. We can speak with a harsh tone, a sarcastic tone, a tender tone, etc. Our tone of voice has a direct connection to the intensity of the conversation. "A gentle answer deflects anger, but harsh words make tempers flare"—(Proverbs 15:1). There is perhaps nothing more directly connected to intensity than tone. Our volume and tone can be water to a small flame, or gasoline. If I cut someone with my words, or raise my voice, or sneeringly address them, I may get to my goal, but at what cost? If I shatter the glass door of a relationship in the pursuit of my objective, what have I really gained?

3. Tact. When the Apostle Paul visited Mars Hill, he addressed a group of philosophers. Prior to speaking, he had toured their city. He noticed many statues and shrines, erected to worship false gods. His goal was to introduce the gospel into that pagan culture. When he stood before them, he could have said, *I noticed you have many idols dedicated to false gods. They are dead, powerless images what will give you nothing. If you continue to worship them you will all burn in eternal hell. There is only one God and He is Jesus.* His words may have been true, but no one would have listened to him. Instead of blasting their false gods, he spoke to them about the true God. Instead of minimizing their belief system, he showed them respect while also sharing the truth of Jesus. Here is his opening statement to them. "As I was walking along I saw your many shrines. And one of your altars had this inscription on it: 'To an Unknown God.' This God, whom you worship without knowing, is the one I'm telling you about"—(Acts 17:23).

If we use tact, are careful about our tone and regulate our tempo, we may not always accomplish our goals, but we will keep from shattering the glass door of relationships. And God cares far more about the glass door than He does the goal. Relationships are the very heart of what God cares about. If He wants us to achieve a goal and we can't get to it without shattering a glass door, God is more than capable of finding another way to that goal without shattering the door. I wish I had known that earlier in my ministry. I cringe to think about some of the relationships I damaged early on. There were people who were not going along with the vision of the church. We were heading in a specific direction and some on the team were not in step with where I felt we needed to go. I shattered too many glass doors. I forced them to go the way I wanted them to go, or kicked them off the team. I let some people go who were in the way. We got to our goal, but the glass door of a relationship was shattered. In the end, I think God cares more about that, than He does whatever goal I was trying to reach. I was using people to get what I wanted, instead of using resources to build people. It was all done in the name of ministry, mission and Kingdom building, but it was more about my egocentric pursuit of a goal. We were about achieving something great, rather than loving people. That's probably my greatest regret from those early years of ministry. Gentleness is the better way. It manifests the life of Christ.

Jesus is the ultimate example of gentleness. When Isaiah prophesied of His coming he said "He will not crush the weakest reed or put out a flickering candle"—(Isaiah 42:3). When Jesus was here, He said, "Come to me, all of you who are weary and carry heavy burdens, and I will give you rest. Take my yoke upon you. Let me teach you, because I am humble and gentle at heart, and you will find rest for your souls. For my yoke is easy to bear, and the burden I give you is light"—(Matthew 11:23-30). Jesus had ultimate power, yet allowed Himself to be nailed to a cross. While hanging there, the people surrounding Him mocked Him and challenged Him to prove He was God by coming down from the cross. I have often thought it's a good thing I wasn't God, for had I been hanging there, I would have come down from that cross and destroyed my tormentors. It's that desire to love, more than to be vindicated that separates Jesus from us mere mortals. The power of His love was stronger than the desire for vengeance.

11
Faithfulness

One of the things I used to do often when I lived in Maine, was walk on the trails of Mantel Lake Park to pray and meditate. One winter day, while making my way through the woods, I rounded the bend in the trail and almost bumped into an owl that was perched on a branch close to the edge of the trail. The huge bird startled me. I jumped back with a gasp, but she was unfazed. She stared back at me with total unconcern. I knew there were owls in that area, but I had never seen one before. The Great Horned Owl lives in that area and can be seen in winter, because they build their nests a full two months before other birds. What they do, is find an abandoned nest from another bird and build on to it, adding twigs and down feathers. They lay their eggs in late winter, and then sit on them without leaving the nest for four weeks. They go without food or water, because in that cold climate, if they leave the nest, the babies will die. The reason they go through the cold and fast for four weeks, is because when the eggs hatch the trees have not yet leafed, and there is usually snow cover on the ground, making it easier to hunt for rodents to feed the ravenous little birds. Baby owls are about three inches in length, but in three months will grow to over two feet tall. They are eating machines. So the mother will brave the cold and go without, in order to feed and nurture her young. God built those instincts into the Horned Owl, and they give us a living picture of faithfulness.

Galatians 5:22-23 says one of the fruit of the Spirit is faithfulness. Faithfulness encompasses a lot of different characteristics—responsibility, dependability, trustworthiness, integrity and loyalty. The word is not easy to define, but we know it when we see it. It is easier to show than it is to tell. So let me show you faithfulness as it's presented in the Scripture in the lives of some important people.

Loyalty When God Is Silent

Faithfulness includes loyalty. In the book of Genesis we read about Joseph. He was one of twelve sons, and he was his father's favorite. The other brothers knew he was their father's favorite. Jacob, their father didn't try to hide that fact. He gave Joseph a special coat that clearly marked him as the special object of his father's admiration far above any of his brothers. The coat signified he would inherit the greater portion of his father's inheritance. That hurt the other sons, because he was the eleventh of twelve. In that culture, the firstborn was privileged to receive the greater inheritance. But Jacob broke the tradition by favoring his younger son. The other brothers were understandably jealous and wanted to get rid of Joseph. Joseph had a dream that one day he would rule over all his brothers and even his father and mother, and in his naivety he shared the dream with the family. They resolved to get rid of him. While away from home, tending their flocks, the brothers grabbed Joseph and threw him into a pit. They sold him as a slave to some travellers, took his special robe and dipped it into blood and told their father, Jacob, they found it and could only assume a wild animal had killed him. Joseph was taken to Egypt and sold as a slave to an Egyptian official named Potiphar. His entire life was taken from him, and God was silent. But in the wake of unanswered questions, he continued to trust a God he could not have understood. Why was this happening? Why didn't God stop it? What about the promises to rule over his family? We may know the end of the story, but he didn't. He worked diligently and faithfully for Potiphar and God favored him. Potiphar prospered with Joseph on the team, so he promoted him as head over his entire household. Perhaps God was still there. But just as it looked like his dreams may come true, they vanished like he was abruptly awaked from sleep. Potiphar's wife found Joseph attractive and tried to seduce him. He protested, stating his allegiance to Potiphar and to God. Once she realized she was getting nowhere with him, she accused Joseph of trying to rape her. Her word against a slave's? Forget it. He specifically told her he could not do this thing because of his faithfulness to God and to her husband. And what did it get him? Prison. And where was God when all this was going on? Silent. But Joseph continued to serve the Lord. It seemed the dreams God had given him were getting farther and farther away, yet he never wavered. He trusted God when nothing made sense. If you know the end of the story, after being in prison for a few years, through providential circumstances, Joseph was finally promoted in meteoric fashion to second in command under the Pharaoh. If I could chose one word to describe Joseph during that time, it would be faithfulness.

Responsible in the Face of Risk

Several years ago, I had the opportunity to travel to Swaziland, Africa. When we arrived, the country was preparing for an annual festival that drew visitors from all over the world. It was called the Umlanga Reed Dance ceremony. Swaziland is led by a king. He is not a figurehead as in some European countries, but is a true sovereign who sits on the throne and makes the decisions for his country. Every year he chooses a new bride to add to his harem. The way he selects his bride, is through the read dance. Women from all over the country will dance before the king and the one who pleases him the most will be chosen as his bride. We did not go to the ceremony because the distinct feature of the reed dance is that the women dance topless. When a woman is chosen to be the king's wife, she is given a palace to live in. This is a great opportunity for young women who mostly are raised in impoverished situations. We were told that the women who are chosen for this will live out the rest of their lives in the palace and will only see the King when he comes to visit them. There are different palaces throughout the country for each of the wives and they live in their own palace but do not visit the rest of the country or see the King until he chooses to visit them. They are literally sequestered away from the rest of the world.

This is not unlike what happened to Esther in the Bible. She went through a somewhat elaborate beauty contest. She pleased the king the most and so she was chosen to be his wife. She too, was sequestered away in the palace and was only allowed to see the King when he called for her. In fact, no one was allowed to see the King unless they were first invited. If someone approached the king without an invitation they literally took their lives in their own hands. If the King held out his scepter to an uninvited guest, they would live, but if not, they were put to death. A plot had been hatched to exterminate the Jews. Esther's uncle, Mordecai, visited Queen Esther and pled with her to speak to the king to try and change the ruling. Esther was reluctant to do anything because she had not been summoned to the King for over 30 days. To show up uninvited was a great risk. Plus, she had not yet told the king that she herself was Jewish. But her uncle challenged her that perhaps the reason God allowed her to come to the throne was for just such a time as this. She agreed to speak for her people even at the risk of her own life. She fasted for a number of days before approaching the King, but when she did, he held out his scepter. Esther is a marvelous story of plot twists and turns, but in the end the Jewish people are saved because of what Esther did. She was willing to take responsibility even though it required great risk. That is faithfulness.

Dependable Under Pressure

Think about Nehemiah who was granted permission by the King to rebuild the walls around the city of Jerusalem. The Jews had been in Babylonian captivity for 70 years while Jerusalem lay in ruins. Finally, they were allowed to return to their homeland. But their beloved city was unprotected without walls. Ancient cities depended on their walls to provide protection from intruders and attackers. Those living in the region were not happy about the Jews coming back into the area and so threatened to oppose their work. Nehemiah and his men were so determined to get the job done they worked with a trowel in one hand and a sword in the other so they would be ready for conflict. He also positioned each person to work on the part of the wall that was directly in front of their own home. That provided great motivation to get the job done. Under opposition and threats they completed the wall in 52 days. Nehemiah was dependable when under pressure. That is faithfulness.

Trustworthy though You Stand Alone

Joshua and Caleb are a part of a contingency of 12 who were sent into the Promised Land on a reconnaissance mission. The Israelites, after wandering in the wilderness for two years, were about to go in and take possession of the land God has promised to their forefather Abraham over 450 years earlier. And now it was time to go in and possess that land. But Moses needed Intel about what was in the land. So he sent in 12 spies to check it out. When they returned they said the land was amazing. It truly was flowing with "milk and honey". But there was a problem. There were giants in the land. They were so huge that the spies looked like grasshoppers in their sight. There was no way they could go in and take land. They might as well turn around and go back to Egypt. Ten of the spies gave that report, but there were two spies, Joshua and Caleb, who said yes the land is beautiful and it flows with milk and honey, and yes there are giants in the land. But God has given us this land and we can take it. They pled with the people to listen to them. They were faithful in their testimony even though they stood alone. But the people rejected their word. And they were forced to wander in the wilderness for another 38 years. So it was 40 years of wandering before they were finally able to enter into the land. During that time all of those spies died off, except for Caleb and Joshua. They lived through the wilderness wanderings, and God honored them for their faithfulness. They were an able to eventually enter into and take possession of the land. They were trustworthy even when they had to stand-alone in an unpopular position. That is faithfulness.

Integrity When it Hurts

Another aspect of faithfulness is integrity. When the presidential elections were going on this last fall, and it became clear that Donald Trump was going to become the front-runner, the opposition began to dig up every bit of dirt they could find on him. Because that's what you do in politics. If you run for political office it does not matter what skeletons you have buried they are coming out. Just about everybody has skeletons, and they will find them. So it wasn't very long before dirt was exposed on front-runner, Donald Trump. Before long, there was a video released of Donald Trump talking with Howard Stern about his sexual conquests. When that news story came out, everyone thought Trump was done. But somehow he survived the political mudslinging. But his people also looked at their opponent, Hillary Clinton, and tried to dig up dirt on her— because that's how you do politics today. You dig up dirt, broadcast it to the public, and hope it will damage your opponent's poll numbers. But of course, that was not so hard to do with Hillary cause everyone already knew about her personal server that she dumped classified documents onto and then had them erased. Trump was able to survive his scandals, but Hillary was not. And so she lost. But regardless of who is running for office their opponents will find political dirt and expose it. And if there is nothing, they will try to either invent it or trap you in something in order to create it. That is what makes the story of a man named Daniel so remarkable. Daniel was a prime minister under the emperor. Daniel had been a Jewish captive but prospered in the Babylonian empire. A Jewish refugee held high political office, and the other politicians under Nebuchadnezzar hated him for it. So they engaged in the age-old tactic of trying to dig up dirt on Daniel, and smear his name to put him out of favor with the king. But no matter how deeply they pried; they could not find anything on him. The only thing they could find on Daniel was that he prayed three times but day. There had been a law passed against worshiping any god except for the king. Daniel's enemies knew he was dedicated to his God and prayed every day. So they used his prayer life to get him thrown into prison. Daniel was thrown in a den of lions because he would not recant of praying to Jehovah. He lived with integrity, even when it hurt. That's faithfulness.

The Character Trait of Faithfulness
vs. the Spiritual Fruit of Faithfulness

Faithfulness encompasses all of those things integrity, loyalty, trustworthiness and dependability. But as I was thinking and praying about faithfulness a question came to my mind. What is the difference between the character trait of faithfulness, and the spiritual fruit of faithfulness? The fruit of faithfulness is it a quality that should be unique to the Christian because the believer possesses the fruit as a result of the presence of the Holy Spirit in their life. Yet if you look at society, you can find many examples of people who are not Christ followers, but they are loyal, dependable, trustworthy and people of integrity. If faithfulness is truly a Christian characteristic then there must be a difference between the fruit of faithfulness and the faithfulness that we see in the lives of many people, regardless of their spiritual background.

The word faithfulness has as its Greek root, the word *pistis*. That root word can be translated as either faithfulness, or faith. Faith and faithfulness are the same word at their root. When we think about faith we often think of it as a mind word. It is an intellectual or doctrinal thing. We speak of the content of our faith. Faith is about what we believe, and why we believe it. If you are a follower of Christ you have to believe the right things. It's all about the content of your belief system. John 3:16 says, "for God so loved the world that he gave His only begotten son that whosoever believes in Him should not perish but have everlasting life." So we are to believe that he is God, that He came to earth and became a man, and lived and died for our sins and rose from the dead. We teach that if we believe those things we will be saved. But there is a problem. The book of James says that demons believe in the existence of God. The gospels reveal that demons even know who Jesus Christ is and referred to Him as the Holy One of Israel and the Son of God. James also tells us that not only do the demons intellectually know who God is but they shutter in His presence. And yet, they are not saved. Faith is not simply about believing the right things. Words evolve over time. When the New Testament was written, the word *pistis* that we translate as faith, did not refer primarily to the content of our belief. A better word to capture its meaning is the word trust. There is a world of difference between belief and trust. I can place a stool in front of you and tell you I believe it exists. We can look at it and see it is an oak color. We see its shape. We can touch it. We mentally agree the stool is there. That's believing. But trusting is something different. To trust the stool means I am actually willing to put my weight on it. I am willing to sit on it and trust it to hold me up.

So when John says that God have His Son so that whoever believes in Him—it does not mean salvation is available to the one who intellectually acknowledges the Christ. What John means is that the one who trusts in Jesus, who places the weight of their life in His hands—that's the one who has eternal life.

The root word for faith is the same for faithfulness. It's this word that refers to trust. So instead of thinking faithfulness, it may be better to think trustfulness. The fruit of the Spirit we call faithfulness is about being full of trust. It is a trust that comes into our lives because of the presence of the Holy Spirit in us. In the Upper Room when the disciples were with Jesus and He was predicting He would die, all of them were boasting about how faithful they would be. They all said even if they had to go to death they would not give up on Jesus. Peter was especially forceful declaring that he would even lay down his life for the Lord. Jesus corrected him and told him that before the Sun rose the next morning he would deny three times that he even knew who Jesus was. When Jesus was arrested they all scattered, just as Jesus had predicted. 50 days later on the feast of Pentecost the Holy Spirit was poured out upon the disciples. Something happened to those disciples. They were transformed. Now they stood before thousands of people, and Peter preached to the very same crowd that had crucified Jesus. The fear was gone. The uncertainty had vanished. He was faithful to proclaim the message of his Lord even though it could very well cost him his life. Every one of the disciples stood courageously for the Lord and tradition tells us that each of them were martyred for their faith. They were willing to go to the place of death because each of them were filled with trustfulness. They did not trust that God would deliver them from danger. Instead, they trusted that God had already delivered them from death.

Jesus' Faithfulness Available to Us

Jesus was filled with trust. He was faithful. 1 Peter 2:23 says, "and while being reviled, He did not revile in return; while suffering, He uttered no threats, but kept entrusting Himself to him who judges righteously." Jesus wants us to live lives of faithfulness because that same spirit of trust that filled Him, fills us. He wants us to be loyal in our lives, even when God is silent. He wants us to be trustworthy even when we have to stand alone. He wants us to be dependable even when we face opposition. He wants us to be responsible even when it incurs great risk. He wants us to live with integrity even when it hurts. Not because God has promised to deliver us from danger, but because God has already delivered us from death. God is faithful and He wants us to be faithful as we allow Him to express Himself through our lives. Lamentations 3:23 says, "Great is Thy faithfulness."

Thomas Chisholm was born in a log cabin in Franklin, Kentucky. He became a Christian when he was twenty-seven, and entered the ministry when he was thirty-six. Poor health forced him to quit the ministry after just one year. He ended up working a desk job for the rest of his life. Because of poor health he struggled not only physically, but financially. Toward the end of his life he wrote, "My income has not been large at any time due to impaired health in the earlier years which has followed me on until now. Although I must not fail to record here the unfailing faithfulness of a covenant-keeping God and that He has given me many wonderful displays of His providing care, for which I am filled with astonishing gratefulness." Chisholm liked to write poetry. One of his poems spoke of the faithfulness of God. It became popular and made its way into the hymnody of the church.[62]

Great Is Thy faithfulness, O God my Father!
There is no shadow of turning with Thee;
Though changest not, Thy compassions, they fail not
As Thou hast been Thou forever wilt be.

Refrain:
Great Is Thy faithfulness,
Great Is Thy faithfulness,
Morning by morning new mercies I see;
All I have needed Thy hand hath provided
Great is Thy Faithfulness, Lord unto me!

Summer and winter, and springtime and harvest,
Sun, moon, and stars in their courses above,
Join with all nature in manifold witness
To Thy great faithfulness, mercy, and love.

Refrain

Pardon for Sin and a peace that endureth,
Thine own dear presence to cheer and to guide,
Strength for today and bright hope for tomorrow
Blessings all mine, with ten thousand beside!

Refrain[63]

12
Peeling Potatoes

There are some people in this world who are what I would consider the epitome of discipline. They are so self-controlled that they excel to extraordinary degrees. Elon Musk is one such individual. He started writing and selling computer code at age 12. At a young age, he sold his company, Zip2, for $300 million dollars. We would know him because he is responsible for the company we call PayPal. It sold for $1.5 billion dollars. He said a large part of his success was his extreme commitment to discipline. He says that early on he recognized there would be trying times. He said he needed to condition himself to be prepared for that so he made the decision to restrict himself to a daily food allowance of one dollar a day. He reasoned that if he could get by on that amount then he could face any challenges ahead without the fear of failure, knowing that if he could make it on a dollar a day he could take whatever risks he needed in business. It was extreme discipline and self-control that brought him to that place.

In the arena of writing, one of the most prolific authors of the 20th and 21st Century is Stephen King. He has written 55 novels and 200 short stories, a number of which have been made into movies. *Carrie*, *The Green Mile*, *The Shawshank Redemption* and *The Shining* are a few notable examples. He made a decision early on in his career. He believed that if he was to be a writer he needed to write, so he disciplined himself to write a minimum of 10 pages a day, every day. And all of these years it does not matter if it was a holiday, his day off, Christmas or even his birthday, he wrote a minimum of 10 pages every day. That is extreme discipline.

In the area of sports, Tiger Woods is a recognizable name to golf fans and even to those who are not interested in the sport. In the 1990s, and the first decade of the 2000s, Tiger Woods was tearing up the golf course. A typical day of golf practice for Tiger Woods, was 2 to 3 hours in the morning on his long game; an hour of putting practice; nine holes of golf; another 2 to 3 hours on his long game; another hour of putting; and then some evenings another nine holes of golf. That is his daily routine—extreme discipline.

Human Discipline vs. the Fruit of Self Control

I was thinking about discipline and self-control because we have been studying the fruit of the Spirit. We have come now to the final characteristic, "but the fruit of the Spirit is… self-control"– (Galatians 5: 23). I got thinking about that—self-control, and about these people in the world who have extreme self-control. And I wondered what is the difference between the self-control they exhibit and the spiritual fruit of self-control. They must be different because the fruit of the Spirit means the Holy Spirit is expressing the life of Jesus through us, which means that characteristic of self-control should be unique to the Christian. It is only that person who is born from above that the Spirit of God comes into him and it gives them spiritual life, and thus the spiritual fruit of self-control. So that somehow has to be different than the self-control we see exhibited in the world. I picked Elon Musk, Stephen King and Tiger Woods precisely because they, though exhibiting extreme self-control, do not profess to be Christian. They are not experiencing the spiritual fruit of self-control, but when we look at their lives, they are more disciplined then most Christians. So what could possibly be the difference between normal human discipline, and the spiritual fruit of self-control?

Democracy Is the Control of the People

The word that is translated as self-control in Galatians 5:23, is a Greek word whose root is the same term that is used for our English word democracy. Democracy means the rule of the people. Is refers to ruling from within, or power from within. Therefore, the spiritual fruit of self-control is talking about the power of God working from within a person to express Himself through that person's life. As we scan through the New Testament we see many verses in the Bible that talk about the idea of the power of God working from within an individual. "For I am crucified with Christ and I no longer live, for the life that I live in the flesh I live by faith in the Son of God who gave himself for me"–(Galatians 2:20). Paul was saying it was not really he who was living, though he was living in the flesh. But the power of Jesus Christ was being expressed through his life because of Paul's union with Christ through the Holy Spirit. In John 7:38, Jesus said, "Whoever believes in me, out of his innermost being shall flow rivers of living water." Then John commented on Jesus's statement in verse 39. He said that Jesus was speaking of the Holy Spirit who had not yet been poured out upon the church. Jesus was clearly indicating that when someone believed in Him the presence of the Holy Spirit would express the life of Jesus through that individual's life like water that was gushing from a spring. The apostle Paul expressed the same idea in Philippians 1:5. "He who began a good work in you will complete it until the day of Christ Jesus." Paul then shared what that would look like in chapter 2, verse 13 when he said, that it is "God who is within you both to will and to work for His good pleasure." What he meant was that God who is within you will produce the desire to do His will and then the power to carry it out. In 2 Corinthians 4:7, Paul said, "We have this treasure in earthen vessels that the greatness may be of God and not ourselves." Paul drew a picture of an earthen clay pot to compare to our lives. We are fragile, brittle, sometimes cracked, but also beautiful and useful. But we have this treasure, the Holy Spirit, that is living inside this common vessel. He chooses to express Himself through cracked pots for the very purpose that it brings glory to Him. No praise can come to us for we are obviously flawed, so any good that proceeds from our lives must be God working through us. Therefore He gets the praise. Jesus said in acts 1:8, "After the Holy Spirit has come upon you, you shall receive Power, and you shall be my witnesses both in Jerusalem, Judea, Samaria and the uttermost parts of the earth."

Be Filled with the Holy Spirit

What the Bible is talking about in all of these instances is being filled with the Holy Spirit. The idea of self-control is the Spirit filling us and controlling the self, living through our lives. So it is not sheer discipline, it is an openness that allows the Spirit to live through us. The apostle Paul, in Ephesians 5:18, said, "do not be drunk with wine wherein is dissipation, but be filled with the Holy Spirit." He was drawing a contrast between getting drunk with wine and being filled with the Spirit. When we think of someone getting drunk with wine we think of them having so much wine inside them that they are controlled by the alcohol. They are not in control anymore, but something else is controlling them. Paul said the person who lives that kind of a lifestyle, constantly controlled by alcohol, lives a life of dissipation. That word is used to describe steam that rises into the air and then quickly disappears into the atmosphere. Their life is like that steam. It is wasted and vanishes away. He contrasts that with the person who is filled with the Holy Spirit. If Paul is talking about being controlled with wine then when he speaks of being filled with the Holy Spirit he likewise is talking about being controlled by the Holy Spirit. So being filled with the Holy Spirit means our lives are controlled by the Holy Spirit. I believe however there is confusion about this. Often when we think of being filled with the Holy Spirit we get the wrong picture in our minds. It is almost unavoidable when we look at the contrast; being filled or controlled with wine versus being filled or controlled by the Holy Spirit. How do you get drunk with wine? You drink it and you fill your stomach with it. By contrast, we think that being filled with the Holy Spirit is similar. Often, we picture in our minds an empty glass and a pitcher of water. The water represents the Holy Spirit and the glass represents our lives. We think to be filled with the Holy Spirit means that the water is poured into our life until we are full. Then we live our lives expending spiritual energy until we are nearly empty. So we have to go back to church to get a refill so we can continue to live with the power of God flowing out of our lives. But I would submit to you that that is an incorrect picture. When Paul was talking about being filled with the Spirit, a word picture that more closely resembles the concept is not a glass, but instead a tube. Picture in your mind a pipe with both hands open. Take that pipe and lay it in a river so that the water flows in one side and out the other. There is a constant flowing of water into the pipe and a constant flow of water out. That is closer to the idea Paul had in mind when he said to be filled with the Holy Spirit. The tense of the Greek verb that Paul used when he said," be filled," is literally translated, "keep on being filled." It speaks of a constant flow through a person's life.

Jesus Emptied Himself

Jesus lived that way. In the book of Philippians Paul said that Jesus emptied Himself when He became human. That does not mean He stopped being God. The second person of the Trinity has always been God, is God and always will be God. Rather it means that He laid aside the independent exercise of His divine attributes. Because He is God, Jesus has all power. But when He came to the earth to live among us, His plan was to not function out of His own divine power. Instead, He would depend upon the infilling of the Holy Spirit. We see clues of this throughout the Gospels. For example, when Jesus was baptized it says that coming up out of the water the Holy Spirit descended on Him in the form of a dove. Then immediately after being baptized, the Spirit drove Him into the wilderness to be tempted by the devil. During those temptations Satan opened the dialogue between he and Jesus with the phrase, "if You are the Son of God..." His temptations were based on the assumption that Jesus was claiming to be God. And if He was, then He should prove it by exercising His power. So the temptation to turn stones into bread was more than satisfying His hunger. He was urging Jesus to exercise His own divine power to change the molecular structure of the stones into bread to feed His hunger and thus prove that He is God. But Jesus wouldn't do it because He had decided that He would not operate out of His own divine power, but would depend upon the filling of the Holy Spirit. The Gospels tell us that after the temptations, Jesus went fourth in the power of the Holy Spirit and did mighty deeds in Galilee. The miracles He worked we're done through the power of the Holy Spirit flowing through His life. He as a human depended upon the infilling of the Spirit to do the works of God. He placed Himself under that self-imposed limitation as an example for us. Jesus told His disciples that they would do greater works than He did because He was going back to the Father and the Holy Spirit was being sent to fill them. It would be easy to look at the works of Jesus and make the excuse that we could never carry out His mission because He is God and could do what He did by virtue of that inherent power. We are just mere mortals and cannot carry on the work of Jesus for we are not God. But Jesus operated as a human dependent upon the Holy

Spirit flowing through His life. His instruction to us was to live the same way. He commanded His disciples to wait in Jerusalem until the promise of the Father, the outpouring of the Holy Spirit at Pentecost. Then they could go forth in the power of the Spirit to do the works of God. So when we are commanded to live the life of Christ we are commanded to live it in the same way. We are to depend upon the power of the Holy Spirit flowing through our lives just as He did through the life of Jesus.

Jesus Saw with Spiritual Eyes

As a result of that, Jesus made the statement that He did not do anything unless He first saw His Father doing it, nor did He say anything unless He first heard His Father say it. In other words He was saying that He was watching what the Father was doing through the Holy Spirit, and then responded to what He perceived God was doing. Understand, that Jesus did not literally see the Father working nor did He literally hear the Father speaking. He saw and heard with spiritual eyes and ears. He discerned the moving of the Spirit in a situation and then He joined what God was doing in that moment. As a result, the release of God's power flowed through His life. That is what it means to walk in the fullness of the Holy Spirit. He lived that way because He had an expectation that you and I would live that way. Jesus did not operate in His own divine power, but walked in a dependence on the infilling of the Holy Spirit, and He is expecting us to live the same way. But how did Jesus do it? How did He perceive the Spirit?

One of the things I noticed about the life of Jesus is that He is extraordinarily perceptive when it comes to people. He had the ability to discern what was going on inside of people, because He carefully observed them. On one occasion Jesus was travelling through Jericho. Hundreds of people were lining the road. They all wanted Jesus' attention. There was a blind man named Bartimaeus who was sitting on the side of the road. He couldn't get close to Jesus because of his condition, but he was crying out, "Son of David have mercy on me." Some of the people standing by him were urging him to be quiet and not make a disturbance. With all the crowds it was a cacophony of noise. Even so, Jesus zeroed in on the blind man. He was aware of the man's need. Jesus stopped and asked him what he wanted and he responded that he wanted to see. Jesus healed him. On another occasion Jesus was walking to the home of a synagogue official to heal his ill daughter. The crowed was so packed, they were pressing against Jesus. A woman had somehow crawled her way through the forest of legs to Jesus and reached up and touched the hem of His garment. At that moment Jesus stopped and asked who touched Him. There were many people touching Him, but He perceived someone reached out to Him in a very special way. Then He turned to the woman who was healed and ministered to her soul. Jesus had an incredible capacity to really see people, to be present with people.

We sometimes think the way to see God is through what I would call emotional goose bumps. When we are in a worship service and the music is just right and we are moved to tears, we often will reflect later that the Holy Sprit was all over that meeting. Sometimes people think the Holy Spirit is seen through mystical experiences like visions or dreams. I am not discounting that there are times when God uses those means. But the far more common way for people to see God is to see people. For example, you may be talking to someone and something that is said stirs him or her emotionally and they react out of character. At that moment we may perceive that God is doing something in that conversation. If we are trained to really see someone, we can see an open door to respond to what God is doing in that moment. When we respond in those God-moments, the Holy Spirit expresses His power through our lives so that we become a minister to that person. That is what the fruit of self-control is all about.

Wax On—Wax Off

But how do we do that? All too often we are so wrapped up in our own lives, focused on our thoughts, our tasks, our agendas that we miss it. How do we train ourselves to really see people? I would like to suggest an exercise you can do that will help you to develop spiritual eyes and spiritual ears. Do you remember the movie from 1984, *The Karate Kid*? The kid asked Mr. Miyagi to teach him how to fight. He showed up at Mr. Miyagi's home, expecting to begin his first lesson, but instead he was handed a rag. He was instructed to apply the wax on Mr. Miyagi's car by rubbing in a clock-wise motion with his right hand, and then rub the wax off in a counter-clock-wise motion with his left hand—wax on, wax off. All day long the kid is waxing Mr. Miyagi's cars—waxing on, and waxing off. He draged himself home at the end of a long and tiring day. When "Danielson" returned the next day he was hoping for a lesson, but instead he was handed a paintbrush with specific instructions on how to apply the paint to the endless line of boards in Mr. Miyagi's fence. After sometime, Daniel was fed up, suspecting that Mr. Miyagi was taking advantage of him and only using him to get chores done around the house. When he confronted Mr. Miyagi, the teacher instructed Daniel to block punches using the motions he learned when waxing his cars. Daniel discovered that Mr. Miyagi was teaching the student muscle memory as Daniel instinctively moved to counter the blows of his teacher. If we are going to learn to really see people, like "Danielson," we have to learn spiritual muscle memory. If we can learn to be perceptive to people, then we can be perceptive to the moving of the Holy Spirit. And if we can do that, and join Jesus in what He is doing, we will experience His life flowing through us to minister to another—we will live out the spiritual fruit of self-control.

Peeling a Potato

Have you ever peeled a potato? I suspect you probably have. If you are like me, when you are peeling, you are trying to get it done as quickly as possible. Often when peeling the potatoes, I am thinking about other things. I'm not really paying attention to the potato. Instead I am either talking with people, listening to the radio or watching TV. I am mindlessly peeling while I focus on something else. But have you ever stopped to really focus on peeling a potato? Next time you peel a potato, block out the entire world and focus in on this one thing. Feel how heavy it is in your hand. Notice how rough the skin is. Watch the skin curl between the two blades of the peeler. Look at how wet the meat of the potato is as you are peeling back the dry skin. Smell the starch in the pulp. You can do that with a potato, or when you are mowing the lawn, or changing your brakes, washing the dishes. Take one mundane task a day and practice concentrating on that task to the exclusion of all other things. Spiritual directors call that being present. It's learning to be present in the moment and focusing on that one thing. Don't let your mind wander or get sidetracked. If it does, don't condemn, or judge yourself, just pull yourself back to that place of laser-focused concentration. Such an exercise seems silly. But it is a form of waxing on and waxing off. It is a way to develop spiritual muscle memory. The practice will remind us of how often we are engaged in something over here, but we're not really here, we are mentally over there. You know what I mean. We are talking to someone, but not really paying attention to anything they are saying. Our minds are elsewhere. If we can learn the simple discipline of being present, it will teach us that when we are with a person (something that is not silly, but of supreme importance) how to be fully there with them and not focused elsewhere. If we learn to be observant with people, then when the Spirit of God is working in that person's life, the Holy Spirit will prompt us to respond and we will get to witness the miracle of the presence of God working through our lives to impact the life of another. When we do that, we are practicing the spiritual fruit of self-control.

Self-control is a capstone to all the other fruit, because love, joy, peace, patience, kindness, goodness, gentleness and faithfulness are dependent on the Holy Spirit expressing the life of Jesus through us. He is love. He is kindness. He is joy, peace, patience and so on. And He wants to express who He is. But He always does it in that pattern. We have to see what God is doing. And the way we do that is to be perceptive to other people. Then when we recognize God doing something in that situation, if we step out in faith and respond to that, His Holy Spirit will empower us by flowing through our lives in the form of the fruit to touch the life of another.

Notes

[1] Though this story is considered a legend, Roger E. Olson testifies to speaking with a retired seminary professor who stated he was at that lecture and heard Barth answer the question. http://www.patheos.com/blogs/rogereolson/2012/12/karl-barths-jesus-loves-me-this-i-know-answer-can-anyone-verify-it/

[2] Hayes, Christopher. Lewis, Huey. "It's The Power of Love." Back To The Future (Original Motion Picture Sound Track). mp3. Geffen Records. 1985.

[3] Rohr, Richard. *The Divine Dance*. New Kensington, Pennsylvania: Whitaker House, 2016.

[4] Turner, Jeff. *Saints in the Arms of a Happy God: Recovering the Image of God and Man*. Clyde Twp., Michigan: Sound of Awakening Ministries. 2014.

[5] Zahnd, Brian. "God Is Like Jesus." *Brianzahnd.com*. August 11, 2011. https://brianzahnd.com/2011/08/god-is-like-jesus-2/.

[6] Milena, Helene. "God Is Christlike." *The Anglican Cathedral of Second Life*. December 27, 2009. https://slangcath.wordpress.com/2009/12/27/god-is-christlike/

[7] Moore, Mark. "The God Who Is Like Jesus." *Mark Moore Blog*. August 22, 2013. https://markmooreblog.wordpress.com/2013/08/22/the-god-who-is-

[8] Devlin, Mike. "10 Insane Facts About The Westboro Baptist Church." *Listverse*. April 18, 2013. http://listverse.com/2013/04/18/10-insane-facts-about-the-westboro-baptist-church/

[9] "Baptist Minister Regrets Orlando Shooter Didn't Kill More 'Sodomites.'" *Haaretz*. December 12, 2016. http://www.haaretz.com/world-news/americas/1.724997

[10] Watts, Craig M. "Mark Driscoll's Badass Jesus." *Church Life*. October 26, 2014. https://www.redletterchristians.org/mark-driscolls-badass-jesus/

[11] Clark, John; Johnson, Marcus Peter. *The Incarnation of God: The Mystery of the Gospel as the Foundation of Evangelical Theology*. Wheaton, Illinois: Crossway. 2015.

[12] Ibid.

[13] Perichoresis Connection. You're Included and Connected. 2017. http://www.perichoresisconnection.org

[14] ibid.

[15] Clark, John; Johnson, Marcus Peter. *The Incarnation of God: The Mystery of the Gospel as the Foundation of Evangelical Theology.* Wheaton, Illinois: Crossway. 2015

[16] Perichoresis Connection. You're Included and Connected. 2017. http://www.perichoresisconnection.org

[17] Hunsinger, G. 2001. *The Dimension of Depth: Thomas F. Torrance on the Sacraments.* In E. Colyer, ed. The Promise of Trinitarian Theology: Theologians in Dialogue with T. F. Torrance. Lanham, MD: Rowman & Littlefield Publishers. Ch. 6. Taken from the God for Us blog. http://martinmdavis.blogspot.com/2011/05/tf-torrance-vicarious-humanity-of-jesus.html

[18] Caleb Smith's sermon titled JESUS LIVED FOR US: THE VICARIOUS HUMANITY OF CHRIST preached on FEBRUARY 5 but posted to his website on SERMONS SEPTEMBER 6, 2016. http://thenicenenerd.com/2015/09/jesus-lived-for-us-the-vicarious-humanity-of-christ/

[19] Cayce was an American spiritualist who lived from 1877 to 1945. He is considered by many to be responsible for popularizing the new age movement. He wrote volumes of pages while in a trance, commenting on ideas as varied as healing, reincarnation and Atlantis.

[20] Gillham, Bill. *What God Wishes Christians Knew About Christianity.* Eugene, Oregon: Harvest House Publishers. 1998.

[21] ibid

[22] Our Faith in Christ or His Faith Within Us? Posted on May 16, 2012 by United Church of God. https://www.ucg.org/bible-study-tools/booklets/you-can-have-living-faith/our-faith-in-christ-or-his-faith-within-us

[23] I heard this concept explained in an interview with Dr. Baxter Kruger on a Grace International Communion podcast titled, You're Included.

[24] Kettler, Christian D. *The God Who Believes: Faith, Doubt and the Vicarious Humanity of Christ.* Eugene, Oregon: Cascade Books 2005.

[25] Moore, Mark. "The God Who Is Like Jesus." *Mark Moore Blog.* August 22, 2013. https://markmooreblog.wordpress.com/2013/08/22/the-god-who-is-like-jesus/

[26] Lewis, C.S. *The Problem of Pain.* New York, New York: HarperCollins Publishers. 1940.

[27] Gillham, Bill. *What God Wishes Christians Knew About Christianity.* Eugene, Oregon: Harvest House Publishers. 1998.

[28] *Celebrate Immanuel's name.* Author: Charles Wesley. Tune: AMSTERDAM (Nares), The first of its three stanzas was published on p126 of Short hymns on select passages of the Holy Scriptures, vol. 2 (Bristol: 1762). The Hymn is Public Domain.

[29] Kerr, Lisa. "Why I Don't Believe In Sin." *My Cult Life: A blog by Lisa Kerr.* June 5, 2016. http://mycultlife.com

[30] Umphrey Lee. *John Wesley and Modern Religion.* Nashville, Tennessee. Cokesbury Press. 1936

[31] Exodus 20:1-17.

[32] Kenneson, Philip D. *Life On The Vine.* Downers Grove, Illinois: InterVaristy Press. 1999.

[33] Winward,Stephen F. *Fruit of the Spirit.* Grand Rapids, Michigan: Eerdmans. 1981.

[34] This is a list I adapted from an online article from http://www.wikihow.com/Stop-Being-Selfish

[35] Scripture fragments taken from Hebrews 1:8-9.

[36] Luke 10:18, 21

[37] Strong, James. *Abingdon's Strong's Exhaustive Concordance of the Bible.* Nashville, Tennessee: Abingdon. 1980.

[38] *The Works of John Wesley, Third Edition Volumes 1 and 2, Journals from October 14, 1735 to November 29, 1745.* Grand Rapids, Michigan: Baker Books. 1996.

[39] Kopstein, Jack. "The Valiant Musicians: World Military Bands." 2011. www.worldmilitarybands.com.

[40] Miller, Ronald E., Durham, Gary L. *One On One Discipleship.* Hyde Park, Vermont: Freedom Ministries Counseling Center. 1992.

[41] Carter, Les. "Mind Over Emotions." *Bible.org.*

https://bible.org/seriespage/lesson-9-envy-green-eyed-tyrant
[42] Angelou, Maya. "Maya Angelou Quotes." *Goodreads.com.*
http://www.goodreads.com/quotes/1208-success-is-liking-yourself-
liking-what-you-do-and-liking
[43] "How To Overcome Envy." *Wikihow.com.*
http://www.wikihow.com/Overcome-Envy.
[44] ibid
[45] ibid
[46] Hedges, Chris. "What Every Person Should Know About War." *The
New York Times.* July 6, 2003.
http://www.nytimes.com/2003/07/06/books/chapters/what-every-
person-should-know-about-war.html
47 "America Has Been At War 93% of the Time – 222 Out of 239
Years – Since 1776." *Washingtons Blog.* February 20, 2015.
http://www.washingtonsblog.com/2015/02/america-war-93-time-222-
239-years-since-1776.html
48 "America's 'startling' use of mental-illness drugs: By the numbers."
The Week Staff. http://theweek.com/articles/480090/americas-startling-
use-mentalillness-drugs-by-numbers.
49 Powlison, David. "Anxiety: How Can I Cope?" *Familylife.com.*
http://www.familylife.com/articles/topics/life-issues/challenges/mental-
and-emotional-issues/anxiety-how-can-i-cope
[50] Swindoll, Chuck. *Anger.* Grand Rapids, Michigan: Zondervan
Publishing House. 1995.
[51] Hawkins, Tim, *Just About Enough*, Rockshow Comedy, Inc. 2016.
[52] Crain, Natasha. "Teachable Moment: Dealing With Impatience."
Christianmomthoughts.com. May 2012.
http://christianmomthoughts.com/teachable-moment-dealing-with-
impatience/
[53] Rohr, Richard. *The Naked Now: Learning To See As the Mystics See.*
New York, New York: Crossroad Publishing Company. 2009.
[54] "Be Still, My Soul", Katherine von Schlegel; trans. Jane Borthwick;
The United Methodist Hymnal, No. 534.
https://www.umcdiscipleship.org/resources/history-of-hymns-be-still-
my-soul

[55] Kenneson, Philip D. *Life on the Vine*. Downers Grove, Illinois: InterVarsity Press. 1999.

[56] Patton, C. Michael. "Believing in God vs. Believing God." *Reclaiming The Mind*. September 25, 2011. http://www.reclaimingthemind.org/blog/2011/09/believing-in-god-vs-believing-god/

[57] "100 Acts of Kindness for Kids January." *Coffee Cups and Crayons*. January 12, 2015. http://www.coffeecupsandcrayons.com/100-acts-kindness-kids/

[58] Powers, Julia. "The Fruit of the Spirit: Goodness." *The Blog of InterVarsity Christian Fellowship*. February 25, 2015. http://intervarsity.org/blog/fruit-spirit-goodness.

[59] Ferguson, Robert. "The Silent Crisis of Mission Drift." *Ferguson Values*. June 10, 2016. http://fergusonvalues.com/2016/06/the-silent-crisis-of-mission-drift/

[60] Lomenick, Brad. "6 Must-Ask Questions to Help Find Your Personal Calling." *Church Leaders*. April 18, 2013. http://churchleaders.com/pastors/pastor-articles/166806-do-you-know-your-leadership-calling.html/2

[61] Lockett, Jon. "Blown To Bits." *The Sun, a UK Company*. August 30, 2016. https://www.thesun.co.uk/news/1694581/trigger-happy-tyrant-kim-jong-un-executes-top-official-with-anti-aircraft-gun-for-falling-asleep-in-a-meeting/

[62] Gaither, Bill: Gaither, Gloria. " 'Great Is Thy Faithfulness'-The Story Behind The Hymn." *Gaither*. http://gaither.com/news/"great-thy-faithfulness"-story-behind-hymn

[63] Chisholm, Thomas. *Great Is Thy Faithfulness*. 1923.